Foreword

Here, at last, is a comprehensive and easy-to-read guide to money aimed at teenagers. A guide that not only covers all the important subjects but also, crucially, makes them interesting.

What we particularly like about this book – here at Nationwide – is the fact that Jonathan Self, its author, shares our philosophy. He believes that consumers should be properly informed, that money need not be boring, and that financial services companies should put their customers' interests first. Additionally he believes, as we do, that it is vital to make the most of every penny of your money.

At Nationwide we don't have shareholders, which means that we put our customers' interests first, including, of course, those customers in their teenage years.

Nationwide

proud to be different

JONATHAN SELF is an author and journalist. He knows about money because he used to run *Self Direct*, one of the UK's largest financial services marketing consultancies, and he knows about teenagers because he has five children of his own aged 11–26. Jonathan is a special adviser to the World Land Trust, an environmental charity. He writes a regular column in *Country Life* and is editor of the personal finance website, *AskSelf*.

The Teenager's Guide To Money

WITHDRAWN

Jonathan Self

For Avery and Laura

Quercus Publishing Plc
21 Bloomsbury Square
London
WC1A 2NS

First published in 2007

A catalogue record of this book is available
from the British Library

ISBN 10: 1 84724 202 2
ISBN 13: 978 1 84724 202 0

Designed by Goldust Design
Printed and bound in Great Britain by Clays Ltd, St Ives plc.

Contents

1

MONEY SECRETS that will set you up for life

1 Why money isn't boring

If you think money is a bit of a boring subject, then consider this.

If you have money, you can do what you want, go where you want and buy what you want. Money is a passport to an easier and more comfortable life. Money means freedom.

In fact, the only boring thing about money is not having enough of it.

Which is why you may find this book interesting.

Because this book is all about how to make sure that you always have enough money.

The most important money secret in the world

Crazy as it sounds, you don't have to be rich to always have enough money.

True, if you earn a huge salary or win the lottery, it will be a great help.

But it isn't vital.

Take an average couple living in the UK. If you add up all the money they are likely to receive during their lives (I am talking about all the money they earn, their pensions when they retire and so forth), it would come to £2 million before tax.

£2 million is a lot of money. Managed properly, it is enough to:

➜ buy a decent home
➜ buy several cars
➜ take dozens of overseas holidays
➜ enjoy all sorts of luxuries like nice clothes and meals out
➜ pay all your regular bills

→ feed yourself and your family
→ retire early
→ build up some savings.

Which brings us to the most important money secret in the world:

Having enough money has less to do with how much money you earn, and more to do with how well you manage your money.

What do we mean when we talk about 'managing' money? Nothing complicated or difficult, just making sure that you:

→ save a certain amount of your money
→ borrow wisely
→ don't allow yourself to be ripped off.

What happens to people who don't manage their money?

Lots of people don't bother to manage their money. For instance, they might:

→ spend every penny and never save
→ borrow and end up in debt
→ pay no attention to what things cost or whether they are getting value for money.

The trouble with this approach is that you can only spend your money once. Even if you are very rich, after your money is gone, it is gone. If you have frittered it away, you won't be able to get it back.

Not surprisingly, people who don't bother to manage their money properly usually end up in the boring position of not having enough. Not having enough money gives you fewer choices about how you live your life. It means things like:

→ working longer and harder
→ living somewhere less nice
→ having less to spend on the things you want.

Not having enough money almost always means worry, too. You may have noticed that the world is full of people who worry a great deal about money.

The sooner you start managing your money, the richer you'll be

The younger you are when you start managing your money, the better off you are likely to become.

This is for the simple reason that in order to make your money grow you need to give it time. The more time you give it, the more it will grow.

Let me give you just one example of this.

Imagine you start saving £1 a day on your 18th birthday. This is what your savings would be worth on your important birthdays up until you reach the age of 60:

At 25 your £1 a day will be worth £3,461
At 30 your £1 a day will be worth £7,362

At 35 your £1 a day will be worth £13,093
At 40 your £1 a day will be worth £21,513
At 45 your £1 a day will be worth £33,886
At 50 your £1 a day will be worth £52,066
At 55 your £1 a day will be worth £78,777
At 60 your £1 a day will be worth £118,025

When you are young, it is quite tempting to think that there is no rush to manage your money. It is easy to imagine that you have plenty of time. But the longer you leave it, the more difficult it will be. Suppose that you want to have savings of £10,000 on your 30th birthday.

➜ You could save 78p a day from the age of 13.
➜ You could save £4.47 a day from the age of 25.
➜ You could save £27 a day from the age of 29.

Every day counts when it comes to making the most of your money, and it is never too early to begin.

Think yourself rich

If you want to greatly increase your chances of having enough money to do whatever you want with your life, then it is crucial to understand that there is a direct connection between:

➜ how you think about money
➜ how you treat money
➜ how much money you are likely to end up having.

This may sound obvious, but you only have to look around to see that many people just don't get it. They lurch from financial crisis to financial crisis because they don't understand their own money beliefs.

Test your own money beliefs

Without necessarily being aware of it, you will already have developed a number of money beliefs. To get an idea of what these may be, read each of the statements below and tick the appropriate box.

		Agree	Disagree	Not Sure
1.	Money is there to be spent.	☐	☐	☐
2.	Money is easy to come by.	☐	☐	☐
3.	You should never borrow money.	☐	☐	☐
4.	Money – and what it buys – can bring happiness.	☐	☐	☐
5.	It is rude to talk about money.	☐	☐	☐
6.	It is important to spend money wisely.	☐	☐	☐
7.	There is nothing wrong with borrowing money whenever you want to.	☐	☐	☐
8.	Having to think about money is tedious.	☐	☐	☐
9.	You should never lend money.	☐	☐	☐
10.	Saving money is a waste of time.	☐	☐	☐
11.	It is sensible to shop around for the lowest prices.	☐	☐	☐

12. Money is a constant worry. ☐ ☐ ☐
13. Making money is satisfying. ☐ ☐ ☐

Now consider your overall attitude to money. How would you describe yourself?

	Yes	No	Not sure
Good with money	☐	☐	☐
Bad with money	☐	☐	☐
Sometimes good/sometimes bad	☐	☐	☐

There is no point in scoring this exercise, because there isn't a right or wrong way to think about money. But certain beliefs are going to make it harder for you to manage your money well. For instance, if you ticked the 'agree' boxes next to the following three statements:

'Money is there to be spent.'
'There is nothing wrong with borrowing money whenever you want to.'
'Having to think about money is tedious.'

then you aren't likely to be doing yourself any money favours.

Make money your friend

So what should your attitude to money be if you want to be better off? In a word: positive. You need to see dealing with money as something enjoyable, something that is worth the effort. It should be part of your life, not a chore.

It may help if you think of money as if it were a close friend:

15

→ Show it respect: don't throw it around or throw it away.
→ Give it time: don't rush money decisions or expect quick results.
→ Look after it: don't neglect or ignore anything to do with your money.

If you know that you are bad with money or erratic (sometimes good and sometimes bad), then the best way to improve your behaviour is to change the way you think.

How to change your money beliefs

Money beliefs tend to be strongly held. This is why people find it so hard to break bad money habits. It is also why money is frequently the cause of arguments between friends, relatives and – especially – couples. This isn't surprising when you think about it. For instance, if one person in a relationship takes a responsible attitude to money while the other person is reckless with it, trouble can't be far behind.

Your attitude to money doesn't come from nowhere. It will be the result of a number of different influences, including:

→ **your money experiences**: if you have had to make do without much money, you are likely to be considerably more careful with it
→ **your parents' attitude to money**: you may share your parents' approach to money or you may reject it, but either way it will influence you
→ **the mystification of money**: there seems to be a general conspiracy to make money as complicated a

subject as possible (it is not helped by the fact that we aren't taught much about money at school)

→ **society's attitude to money**: in Britain it is generally considered rude to talk about money or spend too much time looking after it.

If you want to alter the way you think about money, try to identify the source of your beliefs. Armed with this information, you'll find it much easier to change your attitude.

It is the thought that counts

Human beings, like animals, are creatures of habit. Once we start behaving in a certain way, we often go on repeating it.

Let me give you an example. When I first started work, I used to spend every single penny of my pay within hours of receiving it. I meant to save something, but somehow I didn't. Afterwards I would swear to myself that next week it would be different. But it wasn't.

The more times we do something, the harder it is to change.

What is the solution? If you find it difficult to change the way you are behaving, start by trying to change the way you think.

How can you change the way you think? One method is to repeat the thoughts you want to have over and over to yourself. It sounds silly, but scientists have proved that it works. Another method is to learn everything you can about whatever you are doing because, as a philosopher called Francis Bacon once said, 'knowledge itself is power'. So if you read this book it will help you develop positive money thoughts that, in turn, will help you develop positive money habits.

Don't let money faze you

Money is one of those subjects that people seem determined to make more complicated than is necessary. In fact, pretty much everything you need to know about looking after your money falls into one of four very simple areas. These are:

1. saving and investment
2. borrowing
3. insurance
4. money management.

Understand what each of these four areas involves and you'll find that nothing to do with making money decisions ever fazes you.

Can money make you happy?

Do you wish you had more money? You aren't alone. But would having more money actually make you happy? And, assuming your answer is 'yes', how much more do you actually need? These questions may not be as stupid as they sound.

There are plenty of good reasons to want more money. It is, after all, absolutely essential to our lives. We need it for:

→ **survival:** how would we pay for food, clothes and
   somewhere to live if we didn't have money?
→ **improving our circumstances:** for example, if we
   want an education or to buy our own home, we must
   have money
→ **luxury items:** money pays for all sorts of things – from
   mobile phones and meals out to holidays and multi-
   media systems – that make life more pleasant
→ **looking after others:** we need money to support our
   families, to give to charity and to help other people.

In addition, money offers us a number of extra benefits.
These include:

→ **a sense of security:** it is human nature to worry
   about survival – even wealthy people are sometimes
   concerned about it – and having plenty of money goes
   a long way towards making us feel more secure
→ **respect:** society looks up to people with money – life
   is much easier for them
→ **power:** not only does money buy things, it buys influence – the richer you are, the easier it is to get your
   voice heard where it counts.

As money is so valuable to us, it stands to reason that the
more we have of it, the happier we will be. Or does it?

'Result happiness'

In *David Copperfield*, which Charles Dickens wrote over 150 years ago, the famous character Mr Micawber says:

> *Annual income twenty pounds, annual expenditure nineteen nineteen six, result happiness. Annual income twenty pounds, annual expenditure twenty pounds ought and six, result misery.*

Money was worth a lot more in those days (imagine being able to live on £20 a year!) and people used pounds, shillings and pence (instead of just pounds and pence), but the point being made is timeless:

If you spend more than you earn, even if it is only sixpence, the result is misery. If you spend less than you earn, again, even if it is only sixpence, the result is happiness.

So, according to Dickens, happiness isn't necessarily to do with how much money you have, but whether you live within your means.

The best things in life are free

What on earth could be better than being rich? Here are just some of the things that money can't buy:

→ **Good health:** there is no point in being wealthy if you can't enjoy it because of poor health

→ **Love:** it goes without saying that no amount of cash will make people love you

→ **Friendship:** anyone who likes you only because of your money isn't a real friend

→ **Self-worth:** having money and all that it can buy won't actually make you feel good about yourself – this comes from inside you

→ **Peace of mind:** if you are worried about something, or suffer from depression, having a fat bank balance won't make any difference.

It all comes down to one simple truth: the best things in life are free.

What monkeys have to teach us about money

In the 1930s, an American psychologist called Abraham Maslow was doing experiments with monkeys and noticed something very interesting. If the monkeys were both hungry and thirsty and they were given a choice of food or drink, they always drank first. He realised that this was because monkeys, like people, can live for weeks without food but will die within a few days without water. He then found that if the monkeys were hungry and were offered a choice of food or of spending time with another monkey they liked, they opted for the food. This got Maslow thinking about human behaviour. He concluded that our most important needs are physical – that is to say air, water, food, shelter, clothing and so forth, largely the things we must have if we aren't going to fall ill or drop dead. He then went on to list the other things humans need and in what order. For instance, he suggested that the need to live somewhere safe and secure was more important than the need to be loved. The fascinating thing about Maslow's findings is that only a few of the human needs he identified can be bought with money.

Too much of a good thing

Have you ever eaten so much of something you like that you felt sick? Or played a particular piece of music until you were fed up with it? Or done something you enjoyed so many times that you ended up being bored with it?

It is possible to have too much of a good thing – and this includes money.

Too much money can lead to dissatisfaction, boredom and depression. It can also make people spoilt so that they behave badly – something you may have witnessed.

There is a saying: be careful what you wish for. It is a reminder that you may be sorry if your dreams actually come true. Having enough money to meet your needs and do what you want is obviously wonderful. Having more than enough may not make life any better.

How much is enough?

Warren Buffett, one of the richest people in the world, with a fortune worth roughly $52 billion, lives in an ordinary house, drives an ordinary car and takes ordinary holidays.

He could buy just about anything he wanted – private planes, big yachts, enormous mansions, fast cars, jewellery – but instead he has chosen to lead a relatively simple life and to give most of his money away to charity.

Only a very few people ever have the range of choices open to someone like Mr Buffett. But we still have choice. How much effort will we put into making money? How will we spend it when we start to earn it? Only you can decide what is right for you. However, there is an expression you may like to bear in mind in relation to money: you can't take it with you when you die.

Strike a balance

We must have money to survive. It also makes all sorts of things possible, such as the ability to help other people or live somewhere nice or travel. But there are lots of very important needs – health, love, friendship and feeling good about ourselves, to name a few – that money can't buy. And having too much money may actually make us bored and fed up.

1	The only boring thing about money is not having enough of it.
2	Think of money as a close friend. Respect it. Don't rush money decisions. Look after it.
3	Happiness isn't necessarily about how much money you have, but about whether you live within your means.

2 A very, very short history of money

If you were an early Pacific Islander, you would have used cowrie shells. If you were an Aztec, you would have used cacao beans. If you were an ancient Roman, you would have used salt or, for bigger items, perhaps slaves. Nowadays, of course, we use notes, coins, bits of paper, plastic cards and information technology.

Over the last few thousand years, money may have changed beyond recognition but the reason we need it, and the principles upon which it is based, haven't. Which is why learning about the history of money will help you to make the most of your own.

It began with barter

If you were asked to name some great human inventions, what would you choose? The wheel? Electricity? The telephone? The chances are that you wouldn't mention one of the oldest and most advanced technologies devised by humanity: money.

Money began with barter. A fisherman, for instance, might exchange some of his catch for fruit or a hunter might exchange an animal skin for spears.

The trouble with such a primitive system was that it took a lot of time and effort. You had to find someone who wanted to swap with you and then you had to work out a deal.

So most societies developed what the dictionary calls a 'medium of exchange', which is what we think of as money.

How does money actually work? Let's consider the cowrie shells favoured by the early Pacific Islanders mentioned above. A fisherman living in that part of the world might exchange (or sell) a bag of fish for, say, ten cowrie shells. He might then swap the cowrie shells for all manner of items, as and when it suited him. For instance, he might use three cowrie shells to buy fruit, two cowrie shells to buy meat and one cowrie shell to buy a new grass skirt, keeping four cowrie shells in reserve for later. Cowrie shells obviously make buying, selling and saving much simpler for him. Furthermore, they are easier to carry around and, unlike fish, they won't go off.

Money only works when people believe in it

The whole cowrie-shell-as-money thing can only succeed, of course, if the shells are in short supply. If you could just walk along a beach and pick up handfuls of them, then the whole system would fail. After all, you would have to be a very stupid fisherman to swap your catch for something that was easy to get hold of.

Ever since money was invented, countless governments have been tempted to increase its supply in order to have more to spend. Once paper money became popular, a government could do this simply by printing a bit extra. However, it is not a policy that ever works for very long. As soon as people realise what is happening, the money quickly loses its value. Confidence is a vital factor in any money system.

Money should be measured in time and effort

It is not what money is made from but what it represents that makes it valuable.

Generally, it represents labour. In the case of our early Pacific Island fisherman, he built a boat, made a net and went fishing. So it was his time and effort (his labour) that he was swapping for cowrie shells, and when he spent those cowrie shells it was his time and effort (his labour) he was spending.

To put this in a modern context: if you work for someone in exchange for money, and then exchange the money for food, you are, in effect, exchanging your work for food.

The money itself – whether it is cowrie shells or gold coins – has no real value.

The gold and silver age of money

The connection between money and two precious metals – gold and silver – goes back thousands of years.

The first coins were probably stamped ingots of 'electrum', a mixture of gold and silver, created by the Lydians, a people of Asia Minor, in about 650 BC. The most famous Lydian was King Croesus, who introduced pure gold coins and was the inspiration behind the expression 'as rich as Croesus'. Gold and silver coins rapidly spread in popularity because they made trade – and especially international trade – so straightforward. It was silver coins, for instance, that the Romans used to fund the expansion of their empire. Interestingly, several countries were still minting their coins from silver until the middle of last century.

The Chinese invented the first paper money about a thousand years ago. However, it took several hundred years for the idea to catch on in Europe. It wasn't until 1694, for instance, that the Bank of England began to issue banknotes. One of the interesting things about banknotes is that, until relatively recently, they could actually be exchanged for gold. Indeed, governments were not supposed to issue banknotes if they didn't have sufficient gold in their vaults to give to anyone who wanted to make the swap. Over the last few decades, governments have dropped this idea and now there is rarely any connection between how much gold a country has in its 'reserves' and the value of its currency.

Why aren't banknotes and coins backed by gold and silver any more? Because governments found it incredibly restrictive. A country could be doing really well but, if it didn't have enough gold, this would not necessarily be reflected in the value of its money.

If gold and silver, like cowrie shells, cacao beans, salt and slaves, are no longer used as money, then what is? The answer, as I am about to explain, is: nothing you can actually put your hands on.

We will soon be living in a cashless society

In developed countries, just one-tenth of money takes the form of banknotes or coins. The rest – nine-tenths – is 'electronic money', that is to say it exists only as numbers in bank accounts. So, we have reached a point where not only are banknotes no longer backed by gold, but most money isn't even backed by banknotes. Instead, when one person or organisation wants to pay another, they transfer the 'money' electronically. This money doesn't even exist on paper.

We are moving rapidly towards something that has been

called the 'cashless society'. How long can it be before we stop using cash for anything and instead rely on personal identification numbers (PINs), passwords, 'smart' cards and other technology? Probably not that long.

1	Money is one of the greatest human inventions ever.
2	It is not what money is made from but what it represents that makes it valuable. What it represents is human time and effort.

3 A cunning money plan

What do you want from life? A home of your own? A nice car? Lots of holidays? Enough money to be able to give it away to others less fortunate than yourself?

Thinking much more short term, what would you like? Clothes? Music? The latest mobile phone? An MP3 player? A computer?

Whatever you are hoping for, you need to get yourself from where you are now to where you would like to be.

The fastest and easiest way to get from one place to another is to have a plan. For example:

Imagine you have decided to drive your brand-new sports car through France from Calais to Cannes. You wouldn't just take the first road you saw and hope that it was going in the right direction. You would plan your journey before you set off – perhaps to include interesting sights. If you hit problems (such as traffic delays) during the trip, you would get out your map and find a new route. During your journey, you would check your progress.

A 'money plan' works in exactly the same way. It will help you reach your destination in the shortest time and with the least effort. Plus, it should make your journey enjoyable.

What does a money plan look like?

Your money plan could be as straightforward as a single piece of paper on which you have jotted down a few notes. It is important to write it down, though, so that you can refer to it again in the future. A money plan can be:

→ **for any period of time, from a few days to a few decades:** you might use a money plan for big things (such as buying your own car) or little things (making sure you have enough cash for a special treat next month)
→ **simple or complicated:** you might use a money plan to achieve just one thing (such as making sure you have enough money to buy a computer) or a whole range of things (building up savings for a rainy day, making sure you have money to go to college or even buying your own home).

Anyone, of any age, can (and should) have a money plan

Some people might say that you are too young to be thinking about 'financial planning', which is the technical name for writing a money plan. Rubbish. The second that anyone, of any age, has money of their own, they can and should start planning how best to use it in order to get what they most want. This even applies to a five-year old given a few pence as pocket money.

What should go into a money plan?

The key elements of a money plan are:

→ what you want: what are your money goals?
→ how far you have already got: what is your current situation and how can you best use the money you have?
→ what action you need to take: how are you going to get from where you are to where you want to be?

Start by dreaming

The first step to creating a money plan doesn't involve anything to do with money. Instead, put your mind to what you really want. Write down everything. What are your priorities? Sort your money goals into short, medium and long term. You can't decide how best to organise your money if you don't know what you want to achieve. Here is how Dean, 17, and Alice, 16, did this:

Dean
Short term: 2 CDs, £28.
Driving lessons, £200. Camping holiday with mates, £150.
Medium term: Buy and insure a car, £3,000.
Long term: Move out of home and go to college, £not sure.

Alice
Short term: Clothes for summer holiday, £80. Mobile phone with camera/MP3 player, £110.
Medium term: Laptop computer, £800. Printer, £140.
Long term: Motorbike, £1,200.

When Dean and Alice are older, their dreams may include things like buying their own home or planning for their retirement. What you have to remember is that you can't make a plan of any sort if you don't know where you want to go. Dreaming is a very important part of making money plans.

What have you got to work with?

The second stage of writing a money plan is to assess where you are now and what you have to work with. For instance:

→ Do you have any savings?
→ Do you receive regular pocket money?
→ Do you earn any money, and if you don't, could you start to?
→ Do you own anything you could sell?

Here is what Dean and Alice wrote down on their money plans:

Dean
Savings: None.
Pocket money: Doesn't get any.
Earnings: None.
Things to sell: Unwanted stamp collection, unwanted toys, unwanted bike.

Alice
Savings: £60.
Pocket money: £5 a week.
Earnings: £30 a week from babysitting and ironing.
Things to sell: None.

Obviously, Dean and Alice are nowhere close to having the amount of money they need to make their dreams come true. This isn't unusual. Most people are in the same position. This is where the next stage of the money plan comes in.

Taking action

If you don't have enough money for what you want, you have a choice:

→ give up completely, or
→ rethink what you want, and/or
→ find a way to get the money.

This is what Dean and Alice decided to do when they realised they didn't have enough money to make their dreams come true:

Dean

Dean wants £378 in the short term for some CDs, driving lessons and a holiday with his friends. He wants £3,000 in the medium term to buy his own car and pay for insurance. In the long term he is already thinking about leaving home and going to college. He decides he could:

→ do without the CDs, saving him £28
→ get members of his family to help teach him to drive and take fewer paid-for lessons, saving him £100
→ buy a less expensive car, saving him £1,000.

So now he needs £250 in the short term and £2,000 in the medium term. To raise this money he decides to:

→ start working in a local supermarket stacking shelves at weekends, earning him £60 a week
→ sell his unwanted items on eBay, raising him £100.

Suddenly, his short- and medium-term plans become possible. Within three weeks he should have enough to pay for the driving lessons and a holiday. If he works solidly for a year, he will have more than enough for his car and can start thinking about college.

Alice

Alice wants £190 in the short term to buy clothes and a new phone. In the medium term she wants £940 to buy a laptop and printer. In the longer term she wants £1,200 for a motorbike. Unlike Dean, she is unwilling to change her plans.

She works out that, allowing for her savings of £60, it is going to take her four weeks to earn the money for her short-term needs, another 35 weeks or so to save for the computer and about 18 months until she has the money for her motorbike. While she is working this out, she realises that:

→ she is going to want spending money for other things over this period
→ she hasn't allowed enough money for the motorbike.

So she decides to try and earn extra money by doing more babysitting and ironing.

Be realistic. Be flexible

Your money plan needs to be realistic and should take into account the sort of person you are. For instance, if you are someone who spends, spends, spends, it may be optimistic to imagine that you will be able to save every single penny you get. When you are writing your money plan, allow for things you know you are going to want or need.

A money plan also needs to be flexible. Your priorities may change, or something unexpected may crop up, in which case your plan may have to change, too.

How to save a fortune

There is an incredibly easy thing that you can do to make yourself much, much better off. Shop well.

Let me give you an example.

There are eight shops selling Coke within a few minutes' walk of my house and, depending on which one I choose, I will pay anything from 40p to 69p for a 330 ml can. If I buy a three-litre bottle instead, then 330 ml of Coke will only cost me 17p. If I order Coke in the local pizza restaurant, however, where it is served in tiny bottles, then 330 ml will cost me £2.70p.

In other words, in my immediate neighbourhood, 330 ml of Coke could cost me anything from 17p to £2.70p. So if I want to drink a can of Coke – or its equivalent – I could save myself as much as £2.53p, simply by shopping around.

What is true for Coke is true for most things you buy. Careful shopping can save you a lot of money – money that you can then spend on something else you want.

Making sure you get value for money

Shopping well is really all about getting value for money. 'Value for money' means more than paying the lowest possible price for something you want to buy. Value can come in other ways. For instance:

→ **Convenience:** you might be willing to pay more for something if you don't have to go very far to get it
→ **Quality:** you might be willing to pay more for something if you think it is of high quality (or you might be willing to put up with something of lower quality if it saves you money)
→ **Speed:** if you want something quickly, then you might be willing to pay more for it
→ **Exclusivity:** you might be willing to pay more for something very few other people have
→ **Service:** you might be willing to pay more if you get especially good service.

A good money habit to get into when you are shopping is to ask yourself whether (a) you can get the same thing for less somewhere else and (b) it offers value.

When good sense goes out of the window

People sometimes behave strangely when they are spending money, such as:

→ paying more than they have to for something because they can't be bothered to shop around
→ buying things they don't really want or need
→ spending a lot of time trying to save money on something cheap (like a can of Coke) and then not bothering to shop around for something expensive (like a mobile phone).

If you want to have money to spend on what is really important to you, it is vital that you shop sensibly.

It isn't just about money

Shopping well isn't just about saving your money; it is about saving your time. Suppose, for example, that you earn £3 an hour looking after your neighbour's children. If you spend £15 on a CD in a record shop when you could have bought the same CD in a supermarket for £9, then you aren't just wasting £6. You are wasting two hours (two hours at £3 an hour = £6) of your time. Time you might prefer to spend doing something else.

How to save money when things become a little bit more complicated

Saving money is simple enough when you are buying something straightforward like a can of Coke. This is because there is no difference between one can of Coke and another, so all you have to do is compare the prices to decide which offers you the best value. This sort of comparison is called 'like for like'. Things get a little bit more complicated when you aren't comparing like for like.

A good example of this is when you buy a new mobile phone. In theory, one mobile phone is like another. In practice, you have a huge range of different options open to you:

→ You can sign a contract, which means that you will have to keep the same phone for an agreed period of time but should enjoy cheaper calls.
→ You can decide to 'pay as you go', which involves no commitment on your part but could mean higher call charges.
→ You can take advantage of all sorts of free and discounted offers on calls and text messages.
→ If you do sign a contract, you can take advantage of all sorts of different line-rental and call-charge options.
→ You can choose from a wide range of features, such as camera, personal organiser and MP3 player.

What's more, the products, deals and prices on offer change all the time. What represents good value one day can be expensive the next, and the other way around.

When it is difficult to compare like for like, what you should do is:

→ decide what you really want
→ identify which deals and/or products meet your needs
→ compare the value offered in each case.

What you shouldn't do is allow yourself to be confused by the person selling to you.

Making sure you don't get ripped off

When someone is selling something, there are various tricks they may use to get you to pay more. Here are just five examples of things to watch out for:

1. **Special pricing.** £1.99 sounds cheaper than £2 – especially if you print the 99p so that it is smaller. This sort of pricing trick often fools people into spending more than they mean to.
2. **Loss leaders.** This is where a shop sells something for less than it actually costs them in order to lure you in, because once you are there they hope you will spend money on something else. Supermarkets do

this a lot. Clever shoppers buy the bargains and don't buy anything else.

3. **Something for free.** Nothing is ever free! If you are offered a free gift, it means that the seller is making money some other way. Remember: the customer always pays!

4. **Complicated offers.** Some offers are made complicated on purpose in order to fool customers into thinking they are getting a special deal when they aren't.

5. **Special conditions.** Something can look like a bargain but, in fact, there are all sorts of special conditions (perhaps in small print) that you don't notice until it is too late.

Don't forget, people selling something will always charge as much as they can get away with.

They know that consumers will pay more if:

→ they think they are getting a big discount or something for nothing
→ they are bored (like in an airport)
→ they need something for a particular time (like Christmas or a summer holiday).

Paying for the name

Another way in which people selling things get more for their products or services is by developing a 'brand'. Examples of brands include Adidas, Burberry, Coca Cola, Gucci, Heinz, Kellogg's, Nokia, Nike and Porsche.

When you buy a product with a well-known name, even if it is only a box of cornflakes, you are almost certainly paying more than you would for a product with a less well-known name.

Ten ways to pay less

Here are ten different ways in which you can save money when you are shopping:

1. Shop around comparing prices and value for money. Avoid impulse purchases.
2. Ask for money off or a special deal. It may help to say you are a student or a regular customer.
3. Check whether the same thing is available online for less.
4. See if you can buy what you want for less direct from the manufacturer, wholesaler or from a catalogue.
5. Look on eBay and at the other auction sites to see if you can buy what you want at a lower price.
6. Buy in larger quantities. Usually, the more you buy of something, the lower the price.

7. Accept something slightly different because it is less expensive.
8. Buy 'own' brand, for instance Tesco Cornflakes rather than Kellogg's.
9. Buy second-hand. Pre-owned things usually cost a lot less.
10. Make sure you really want it. Maybe you can make do without.

1	A money plan will help you get what you want from your money in the shortest time and with the least effort.
2	Dreaming is a very important part of making money plans.
3	Careful shopping can save you a lot of money – money that you can then spend on something else you want.

4 The language of money

'Gearing' has nothing to do with cars. It is a way of turning a small amount of money into a very, very large amount of money. For instance, with gearing you might turn £100 into £1,000. It is also a perfect example of one of the most off-putting things to do with money: the language.

Like any other area of life – for example computers or music – money has its own language, or jargon.

Jargon is useful, of course, if you understand the words involved but confusing if you don't.

Which is where this chapter comes in. Because it takes the most important and frequently used money terms and explains them in plain English. In fact, once you read this chapter you will know more about financial terminology than the vast majority of people in the UK. Money words you'll understand the meaning of include:

→ percentages
→ interest
→ compound interest
→ inflation
→ capital
→ income
→ gearing.

Once you understand these words, you'll be in a considerably better position to make more money from your money.

Words to stop you being ripped off

There is another reason to learn a few key money words: it will be much harder for anyone to take advantage of you. When you come to make financial decisions and to buy financial products, you'll find that understanding all the jargon will ensure you aren't ripped off.

Getting to grips with percentages

Speaking of being ripped off, one way to prevent it is to make sure that you are getting value for money. And one way to make sure you are getting value for money is to make sure you know how to work out percentages.

The word 'percentage' literally means 'parts per 100' – *cent* comes from the Latin word for '100'. Because percentages always deal with parts per hundred, they allow you to compare things that would be very difficult to compare otherwise. They are particularly useful when it comes to deciding whether something is better value (or more profitable) than something else.

When we want to write 'percentage' quickly, we use the symbol %.

How do percentages work? The first step is to take the numbers involved and turn them into a fraction. Next, you divide it out. Finally, you multiply by 100.

Let's look at a really simple example. You have 25 bars of chocolate. Of these, 22 are Mars Bars. How can you express this as a percentage? The fraction is:

$$\frac{22 \text{ (Mars Bars)}}{25 \text{ (total number of bars of chocolate)}}$$

When you divide this out (22 divided by 25), you get the answer 0.88. When you multiply it by 100, you get the answer 88. So 88% of the bars of chocolate are Mars Bars.

Let's look at a more useful example.

Imagine that you have three apple trees and want to know which one of the trees produces the highest number of good – as opposed to rotten – apples. When you harvest the apples from each tree, you keep a note of the total number of apples picked and the number of apples that have to be thrown away. Your note looks like this:

Tree	Apples on tree	Rotten apples
A	750	150
B	550	88
C	670	101

Clearly, from the above figures it isn't easy to gauge which is your best tree. However, if you express the figures in percentage terms, it will immediately become obvious.

On Tree A, 150 out of the 750 apples were rotten. So your calculation would look like this:

$$\frac{150}{750} \times 100 = 20\%$$

If you were using a calculator, you would key it in like this:

$$150 \div 750 = 0.2 \times 100 = 20\%$$

For Tree B, 88 apples out of the 550 were rotten, so the calculation would be like this:

$$\frac{88}{550} \times 100 = 16\%$$

For Tree C, 101 apples out of the 670 were rotten, so the calculation would be like this:

$$\frac{101}{670} \times 100 = 15\%$$

Converting the numbers to percentages allows us to make a fair comparison of the performance of the apple trees. Of the apples on Tree A, 20% were rotten; 16% of the apples on Tree B were rotten; but just 15% of the apples on Tree C were rotten – making it the best-performing apple tree in the orchard!

It is hard enough comparing apple trees with apple trees – but even harder to compare apple trees with, say, orange trees. This is where percentages come in so useful. By giving everything a base of 100, we can compare things that aren't alike in other ways.

Interesting, very interesting

The money term 'interest' is used to mean one of two things.

First, it is used to describe the money you earn when you

invest in a bank account or some other sort of financial product. For instance, if you put £100 into a bank account and the bank paid you £5 a year, this would be called '£5 interest'.

Secondly, it is used to describe the money you pay if you take out a loan. For instance, if you borrow £100 and the bank charges you £10 a year, then this would be called '£10 interest'.

You will have noticed that in the two examples I have just given, you pay more interest to borrow £100 than you will earn if you invest £100. This is how banks make their money.

Interest is normally expressed as a percentage. If you invest £100 and get £5 a year in interest, this is called '5% interest'.

The genius of compound interest

When you are earning it, it has the power to make you very rich. When you are paying it, it has the power to make you very poor. Albert Einstein described it as 'the greatest mathematical discovery of all time'. It is the reason why banks, building societies, credit-card companies and other financial institutions make so much profit from lending money. And it is the reason why ordinary investors can make themselves rich simply by doing nothing. It is a fiendishly simple concept called 'compound interest'.

Perhaps the easiest way to understand compound interest is to look at a hypothetical example.

→ Imagine that you have £100 and that you invest it in a bank savings account that pays interest at a rate of 10% per year.
→ At the end of one year, you will be entitled to £10 interest.

→ If you withdraw the interest (in other words, take it out of the bank) but leave your original £100 untouched, at the end of the second year you will be entitled to another £10 interest.

→ Supposing, however, that you don't withdraw the interest but leave it to 'compound', or grow. At the end of your first year, your £100 is worth £110. At the end of your second year, you will have earned another £11 interest, meaning that your original £100 is worth £121 (£100 + £10 interest = £110 after one year. £110 + £11 interest = £121).

→ Put another way, your interest is earning you more interest.

In other words, when you leave your money to earn interest – and then leave your interest to earn more interest – that's compound interest.

When you invest money and leave it to earn compound interest, it grows much, much faster. If you were saving £50 a month for 10 years at 8% a year, and you left the interest to compound, you would have £9,208. Not bad, considering you would only have put in £6,000.

Remember, though, that when you borrow money compound interest is working against you. Why? Because you are paying interest on the interest you owe. Suppose, for instance, you borrow £1,000 on a credit card at an interest rate of 15% – which isn't high by today's standards. The credit-card company allows you to make a minimum payment of £5 or 2% each month – whichever is the higher – and this is what you do. Not only will it cost you £550 in interest to repay your debt this way, but also it will take you a staggering 9 years and 10 months to do so.

Compound interest is your biggest money enemy and your biggest money friend. When you are in debt, it works against you. But when you have money to invest, you can make compound interest really work for you.

Inflation: a few words of warning

What your money can buy changes all the time. In 1981 a Mars Bar cost 15p. In 2006 a Mars Bar cost 44p. Why should this be? What difference does it make?

The word used to describe increases in prices is 'inflation'. There are different sorts of inflation. House-price inflation is when houses cost more than before. Wage inflation is when people have to be paid more. General inflation is when pretty much everything – especially shopping – costs more. All inflation is measured in percentages.

At the moment inflation isn't really an issue. Prices do go up every year but only by a tiny percentage.

In the past, though, inflation has sometimes gone mad. There have been years when prices have gone up by 10% (in other words, something costing £1 costs £1.10 just 12 months later) and more.

When this happens, your money is obviously worth less. This is quite important when it comes to your general level of wealth. If, every year, the value of your money is being eaten away by inflation, you could quickly find yourself much less well off. This is particularly true with regard to your savings. If a bank is paying you 3% a year interest but inflation is running at 2.5%, your money is only growing in real terms by 0.5% a year. Not much!

When you make any money plans for the future, you ought to bear in mind the effect of inflation.

What is capital? What is income?

One of the most important money concepts to understand is the difference between 'capital' and 'income'.

Capital is something – it could be money, a property, shares or some other investment – that generates an income for whoever owns it.

A good way to remember the difference is to think of a fruit tree. The tree itself is the 'capital'. The fruit it produces is the 'income'. You continue to own the tree (capital) and it continues to bear fruit (income) every year. Your wage or salary is the income that comes from the capital of your labour – hence the expression 'human capital'. Money is not just money – it is either capital or income.

When you own capital and it produces an income, you have a number of choices:

→ You can hold onto the capital and spend the income.
→ You can hold onto the capital, add the income to it (turning it into more capital) and generate even more income.
→ You can spend some or all of the capital and thus reduce the income you receive.

There are lots of different names for the income produced by capital. In the case of property, for instance, it is called 'rental income'. In the case of a cash deposit in a bank, it is called 'interest' (see above).

Letting other people make you rich

Using borrowed money to buy an 'asset' (something that can make you more money) is called 'gearing'. If you can make it work in your favour, gearing can dramatically boost your profits. For instance:

Suppose you buy a £100,000 flat using £10,000 of your own money and a £90,000 home loan. After one year, the flat is worth £130,000. It isn't just that you have made a £30,000 profit – you've actually trebled the £10,000 you originally invested. In other words, you've achieved a 300% gain in just 12 months.

Even if you allow for the cost of borrowing the £90,000 for a year, you have still done very well. However, what goes up can also come down. In the UK between 1987 and 1989, house prices fell by around one-third. If this happened to someone selling a flat they bought for £100,000 using a £90,000 mortgage, they would not only have lost their £10,000 deposit but also owe an additional £23,333 or so (the difference between the home loan of £90,000 and the £66,666 they can sell the flat for). When this happens, it is called being 'in negative equity'.

Gearing is the easiest and most effective way of increasing the potential profit from any investment. It is also the most effective way of increasing the potential loss, something every investor thinking of gearing would be well advised to remember.

Without gearing, most people would never be able to own their own homes. It can also allow them to make other profitable investments. Nevertheless, you should think carefully before you make any investment that requires you to borrow money. You want to make sure that the investment is going to earn you more than the loan is going to cost you to repay.

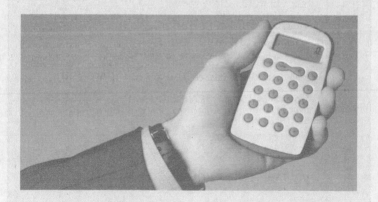

Don't trust your calculator

When you are working out things like percentages, don't always believe the answer the calculator gives you. Why not? Because the tiniest slip of your finger could give you a completely wrong answer without you being aware of it. Here are five things you can do to avoid calculator error:

1. Estimate your answer before you begin a calculation.
2. Do every calculation twice.
3. Know your calculator.
4. Don't be overawed by your calculator.
5. Hang onto common sense and what you know.

1	Once you understand the concepts explained in this chapter, you'll be in a considerably better position to make more money from your money.
2	Percentages allow you to compare things that would otherwise be very difficult to compare.
3	Compound interest allows you to make yourself richer without doing a thing.
4	Gearing – using borrowed money to make money – can dramatically boost your profits, but is sometimes risky.

5 The 'B' word

Down through the ages, people have had different ideas about how to get their hands on extra money without having to work for it. Alchemists have attempted to turn base metals, such as iron or copper, into gold. Explorers have searched for lost treasure. Prospectors have hunted for precious minerals and jewels. Counterfeiters have tried to mint their own coins.

They might all have saved themselves the trouble by budgeting.

Budgeting is a way of taking what you already have and making better use of it.

The result is less spectacular than, say, finding a pirate hoard but considerably more certain. In fact, if you budget properly, you are guaranteed to make your money go much further.

What is a budget?

A budget is nothing more than a plan for how you will spend your money over a specific period of time. You might budget for a day, a week, a month or a year. To produce a budget, all you have to do is work out:

→ how much money you have coming in (and when)
→ what you want to spend it on (and when).

The secret to a successful budget is simply to make sure that you don't spend more money than you can afford or, better still, that you have something left over at the end of the budget period.

How can something so simple actually work?

Why do budgets make your money go much further? The main reason is that the process of budgeting will stop you from:

→ spending money you don't have
→ wasting money on things you don't really want or need.

Budgeting will help you focus your mind on what you have to spend and what is really important to you.

Because you are planning ahead, you are less likely to find yourself short of cash. You are also less likely to worry about money.

A sample budget for a student

Let's look at a sample monthly budget for a student who has just started at university.

Monthly income:	
Part-time work	£400
Grant	£360
Parents	£100
Total income per month	**£860**

Monthly outgoings:	
Rent	£300
Gas, electricity etc.	£50
Food	£200
Household items	£20
Drink	£100
Fares	£30
Mobile phone	£40
Spending money	£100
Total expenditure per month	**(£840)**
Total left over	£20

The brackets, by the way, are used to mean a 'minus' figure. In other words, you have to minus or subtract the sum. In this case, the student has £860 coming in every month but is spending £840. So, although things are tight, he does have £20 to spare.

Five budgeting tips

Here are five budgeting tips:

1. It is a good idea to allow a bit extra for unexpected expenses. Suppose you have to replace something that gets lost or broken. Or you suddenly find you need to buy new shoes.
2. You also ought to allow for those bigger expenses that don't come up every month. For instance, annual

memberships, car or motorbike insurance, Christmas
presents and so forth.

3. Another good idea is to save a little money every month.
As we will see in future chapters, it is the best way to
build your wealth.

4. If you spend more money than you really mean to, then
keep a money diary. Every time you spend anything,
write down what it was for and how much it cost. This
simple process will help you discover where your cash is
going and will highlight where savings might be made.

5. If you find that your income is not high enough to meet
all your expenses, then you have a choice. Either work
out some way to make extra money or cut your costs.

How to keep track of your finances

The best way to keep track of your finances is to
keep a note of all your income and expenditure.

I asked my son, Bert, to do this for a month and
this was the result:

This is money he had coming in.

This was left over from the month before.

Total £77 + opening balance of £4 = £81.

Income

	£	£
Opening balance	£4	
7th June: pocket money	£10	
11th June: babysitting	£12	
14th June: pocket money	£10	
18th June: gardening	£16	
21st June: pocket money	£10	
23rd June: babysitting	£9	
28th June: pocket money	£10	
TOTAL	£81	

Expenditure	£	£
7th June: trip to cinema		£13
12th June: magazines and sweets		£6
14th June: top up phone credit		£10
19th June: computer game on eBay		£11
24th June: birthday present for Jane		£14
28th June: meal out		£16
TOTAL		£70
Closing balance		£11

This is money he spent.

This is what he had left over.

Keeping a note like this tells you:

→ how much you had at the start of the month
→ the different amounts of income you received during the month
→ the total income you received during the month
→ all the different ways you spent money during the month
→ the total amount you spent during the month
→ how much you had left at the end of the month.

1	Budgeting is a way of taking what you have and using it more effectively.
2	A budget is nothing more than a note of what you have coming in (your income) and what you have spent it on.
3	Budgeting can stop you worrying about money.

2

THINGS YOU NEED TO KNOW about money before you reach 20

6 The ultimate guide to banking

A very useful thing, a bank account. Without costing you a single penny, it can provide you with a quick and easy way to:

→ keep your money safe so that it doesn't get lost or stolen
→ get your cash when and where you want it
→ pay for things you want to buy, whether you are shopping in person, over the Internet or from a catalogue
→ pay all your bills
→ send or give money to anyone, anywhere in the world
→ keep track of your money and manage it better.

What's more, banks will do all sorts of other things for you, such as:

→ provide you with foreign currency when you go abroad
→ lend you money
→ help you to make your savings grow
→ top up your mobile phone account.

Banking without ever going into a bank

You don't have to open a bank account with a high-street bank. They are also available from online banks, building societies and even through the Post Office.

So, when I refer to banks, what I really mean is 'banks, online banks, building societies and post offices' – only it is too long-winded to write out every time.

How can you make the most out of banks and bank accounts? This chapter explains:

→ how bank accounts work
→ what you should look for in a bank account
→ all the different services you can get from a bank.

Plus it will show you how to claim all sorts of free gifts (such as CDs, DVDs and personal organisers) and even how to get your hands on some juicy cash bonuses. In short, this chapter is the ultimate guide to banking.

Money problems? Money solutions!

Most things that are bought or sold can be described as either a product or a service. Products are actual things you can touch and use. Services are when someone does something for you. For instance, a mobile phone is a product but the calls you make on it are a service.

Where am I going with this? The money business is called the 'financial services industry'. All the companies that work in this business – banks, building societies, credit-card suppliers and so on – are called 'financial service providers' or 'financial institutions'. And (slightly confusingly) all the financial services they sell (bank accounts, for example, or credit cards) are called 'financial products'.

Each financial product exists, of course, to solve a particular money problem. Here are a few examples:

Problem: Getting cash to a friend abroad.
Solution: International money transfer.

Problem: How to pay for college.
Solution: Student loan.

Problem: How to buy first car.
Solution: Savings account.

There may be more than one solution to a problem. For instance, if you want to invest your money to make more money, there are dozens of options.

Why banks want your business

Many of the UK banks have special deals for teenagers and students, which you can take advantage of if you open an account. The deals include:

→ free gifts, such as magazines, CDs and DVDs
→ cash bonuses
→ free banking.

The free banking might not sound very exciting. According to a recent survey, however, the average customer pays £140 a year – or more – on banking services, so free banking could be worth more than you imagine.

Why are the banks so keen to win your business? Most people don't shop around for banking services.

Once you open an account with a particular bank, the chances are you will stay with them, possibly until you die.

In the short term – until you start earning money – your bank won't make any profit from you. In fact, it will cost them money to look after your banking. But later, when you need other banking services, your bank will hope to make a profit from your business.

Banks give you such a great deal as a teenager or student because they are thinking about the future. They hope that by looking after you now they will keep your custom when you are older.

Choosing a bank account

Banks offer teenagers basic savings accounts that then morph into more advanced accounts when they turn 16 or 18 (for legal reasons there are certain facilities that can't be given to anyone under 18).

What you want, as soon as possible, is a current account. Current accounts are designed to provide you with day-to-day banking and should offer you all the following facilities:

→ a safe and secure place to leave your money until you want to spend it
→ access to your cash via branches and cash machines
→ a simple and easy way to pay your bills
→ a detailed record of all your day-to-day financial transactions.

In order to provide all this, the typical current account will offer you some or all of the following services:

→ a chequebook
→ a cheque-guarantee card, making your cheques (up to a certain value) as good as cash in the hands of the recipient
→ an ATM (this stands for Automated Teller Machine) or cash card allowing you to get cash 24 hours a day
→ a direct-debit facility so that you can pay your bills automatically
→ a standing-order facility allowing you to make regular payments
→ a debit card so that you can arrange direct payments without having to write a cheque
→ bill payment for general bills
→ regular statements
→ overdraft facilities
→ online banking
→ telephone banking.

Your current account may also offer you other facilities. For instance, you may be able to get cash from a supermarket or post office.

Banking terms made easy

Here is a plain-English guide to all the words used by banks to describe the services they offer.

Cheques

You have probably seen cheques and chequebooks. But in case you haven't, a cheque is a special form on which you write an instruction to your bank to pay someone a specific amount of money out of your account.

For example, if you wanted to pay £20 to Reckless Records you would write a cheque for £20 and give or post it to them.

Cheques come in books (usually of about 25 cheques) supplied by your bank. Here are a few tips about cheques.

→ Obviously, the bank will only 'honour' (pay) the cheques you write if you have the money in your account.

→ Many people won't take a cheque from you if it isn't accompanied by a cheque-guarantee card (see below).

→ Cheques usually take about three working days to be 'cleared' (paid). So if you give someone a cheque on a Monday and they pay it straight into their bank account, they will get the money on the following Wednesday or Thursday.

→ Normally, you would date the cheque on the day you write it. But if you want to delay the payment you can write a date some time in the future. This is called a 'post-dated cheque'.

→ When you go shopping, you will probably find using a debit card (see below) a lot easier than writing a cheque.

→ You should always make a note of whom you have written the cheque to, the amount and the date on the cheque stub (the bit of the book that is left after you have torn out the cheque) so you have a note of it for your records.

→ If someone gives you a cheque, you will have to pay it into an account unless they arranged with their bank that you could turn it into cash. This is called 'cashing a cheque'. If you write a cheque to yourself and take it into your own bank to get cash, this is also called 'cashing a cheque'.

Cheque-guarantee cards

Suppose someone writes you a cheque and there isn't enough money in their account to pay it. This is called 'bouncing' a cheque. To overcome the problem, banks offer trustworthy customers cheque-guarantee cards. If the number from this card is written on the back of the cheque, then the bank guarantees to pay it, providing it is under the amount it states on the card. This is usually £50, £100, £200 or £250. When your bank gets to know you, they will probably offer you a cheque-guarantee card. Shops, restaurants and so forth usually won't accept a cheque without a guarantee card.

Automated Teller Machines (ATMs)

An Automated Teller Machine (ATM) allows you to take cash out of your account using a special card. These ATMs, or cash machines, are to be found inside and outside banks, and also in public places like petrol stations and shops. Here are a few tips about cash cards.

→ Most cash cards work in most cash machines BUT some machines will make a charge if you use them, especially when you are abroad. This charge will come out of your account. Your own bank probably won't charge you if you are a teenager or a student.

→ There will be a limit to how much cash you can take out on any given day (from midnight to midnight). The card will have the amount printed on it.

→ To access your cash you will need a special number called a Personal Identification Number, or PIN. See below for more details

→ The smallest amount you can usually take out is £10.

→ Most cash machines will offer you a receipt. You should take this to help you keep track of your money.

Personal Identification Numbers (PINs) and passwords

In order to access cash machines, online banking and telephone banking, you will be sent a Personal Identification Number (PIN) – normally a four-digit number and/or a password – by your bank. You can change the

PIN the first time you use your card to something more memorable.

You should keep your PIN and/or password secret and should follow the security instructions you will be sent.

Standing orders

A standing order is exactly that – a regular ('standing') instruction ('order') to your bank to make the same payment to the same person or organisation on an agreed date. For instance, you might order your bank to pay £10 a month to cover the cost of a sports club membership. Or, for that matter, you might instruct them to pay a much larger amount every other month, every quarter (three months), every six months or every year. You can instruct them to do this until further notice or until a date you specify. If you want to arrange a standing order, you should ask your bank for a special form.

Direct debits

A direct debit is an instruction to your bank to pay a regular bill on your behalf. For instance, you might sign a direct debit instructing them to pay your phone bill every three months. With a direct debit, you don't specify the amount that is going to be paid. Because of this, there are some very strict safeguards in place to protect you. One of these is that only reputable organisations are allowed to use the direct-debit system. Another is that you must receive the bill to be paid at least ten working days before the money is to be taken from your account. Direct debits are a great way to pay regular bills because they save you time and effort. If you want to arrange a direct debit, you should ask your bank for a special form.

Debit cards

Debit cards are another way of buying things, paying bills and getting cash. The agreed amount of money is taken from your account and transferred to the firm or organisation you are paying. You can only make a payment by debit card if you have enough money in your account or if your overdraft credit is large enough to meet the payment. Many debit cards also double as cash cards. Thanks to debit cards, you no longer need to take cash when shopping. You can't use debit cards to pay individuals. They are mostly used to pay online and in shops.

Bank statements

To help you manage your money, your bank will send you a regular bank statement. This will contain details of all the money paid into your account ('deposits' or 'receipts') and all the money paid out ('withdrawals' or 'payments'). You can request statements every month, every two months, every three months or every six months. You can also ask for a 'mini' statement while using a cash machine. It is often possible to see your statement online if you use your bank's online-banking facilities. A balance with a minus sign (-) in front of it means your account is overdrawn (see below).

Overdrafts

An overdraft is a short-term loan offered by your bank as part of your current account facility. You have to be 18 before you can have an overdraft.

→ **An 'authorised' overdraft** is one that has been arranged in advance, though you don't neces-sarily have to use it. The bank normally charges for agreeing this 'facility'.

→ **An 'unauthorised' overdraft** is where the bank decides that, despite the fact that you have no agreement to borrow from them, they will still make some payment on your behalf. Unauthorised over-drafts will cost you a lot of money in bank charges.

Online and phone banking

Almost all the banks offer an online- and/or phone-banking service. This allows you to do all sorts of useful things, like pay bills, transfer money and get a state-ment, via a computer or telephone. For security reasons you should only use online banking if you have your own computer. Using college or Internet café computers could be risky. Ask your bank for details.

Paying money into your account

You can pay money into your account in a number of different ways. You can:

→ Take your money into a branch of your bank (and possibly a branch of other banks, depending on whom you bank with) and pay it in 'over the counter'.
→ Put your money into a special envelope and leave it in a safe or special machine in the branch.
→ Post cheques – but NOT cash – to your bank.
→ Give anyone who wants to pay you money details of your account and ask them to make a direct transfer from their own account. Lots of people get their wages paid this way.

When you pay money into your account, it is called a 'deposit'. Sometimes you will have to fill in a special form when you make a deposit. You will find these forms in the bank branch, in the back of your chequebook and/or you will be given a supply by your bank.

Other ways to pay bills or give people money

You can pay bills or give someone money by transferring the cash directly from your account to the account of the organisation or person you wish to pay. To do this you will have to make arrangements with your bank and will need the account details of the organisation or person you want to pay. You may be charged for this service, so you should check first.

Some bills come with a tear-off bank transfer slip at the bottom. This allows you to pay the bill at your bank or – usually – any post office.

Other ways of taking money out of your account

We have already seen how you can take money out of your account by writing a cheque or using a cash or debit card. It is also possible to take money out (or 'withdraw' it) from your own bank by using a withdrawal form. You can do this at the branch where you keep your account without making special arrangements. If you want to do it at another branch, you may need to make arrangements beforehand.

Bank drafts

A bank, or banker's, draft is a way of paying someone a large amount of money without having to give him or her cash. For instance, if you buy a car, you might pay for it with a bank draft. It is as good as cash to the person receiving it (unlike a cheque, where they have to wait three days to make sure it is paid). You can buy bank drafts from your bank if you need them.

Choosing a bank

There are, literally, dozens of different banks and building societies to choose from. How do you decide which one will suit you best? Here are some tips:

→ Consider going to the same bank as your parents or guardians. You should get better service.
→ Consider opening your account with a building society. Building societies are owned by their customers and use all their profits to improve the service they offer. Building societies were originally set up to help ordinary people buy their own homes. On the whole, they are very good places to keep your money. They tend to charge their customers less and are a bit fairer.
→ Consider the Co-Op Bank, which is also owned by its customers.
→ Weigh up the real value of all the different free gifts, vouchers and cash bonuses being offered to you. Some people open lots of accounts just to get these free gifts, and there is nothing to stop you doing this if you can be bothered. But don't let the freebies blind you to the account features. You need an account that gives you what you want.
→ Choose a bank that is easy to get to. You don't want to have to make a long journey every time you need to do a bit of banking.
→ Check that you aren't going to be charged anything for using the different bank services. While you are still a teenager or student, you shouldn't be paying anything for your day-to-day banking.

It is usually easiest to open a new account in a branch. But it is possible to open an account online or, in some cases, over the telephone.

Proving who you are

When you go to open a bank account, you will be asked to prove who you are and where you live. This is partly to stop criminals and terrorists from using bank accounts under fake names and partly to ensure no one pretends to be you in order to steal your money.

You will need one document to prove who you are and one to prove where you live. Every bank has its own rules about the sort of documents it wants to see, but usually they are things like a passport, birth certificate, paid bill and so forth. It will speed up the account-opening process if you check this first.

Make sure all your banking is free

While you are a teenager, a student or indeed just starting out, it should be possible to enjoy free banking. Some banks will continue to offer free banking for much longer. Free banking is worth having! The average bank customer pays £140 or more a year in bank charges.

How banks make money (and why you need to know)

It is worth remembering that banks are really only shops offering financial or money services.

Although banks charge a large percentage of their customers for current accounts, they don't really make their profits from providing day-to-day banking. This is because it is incredibly expensive running branches, looking after customers and handling billions of pounds of cash every day.

Where banks make their real profit is by selling their customers a wide range of other financial services, such as loans, mortgages and credit cards.

Once you turn 18, every time you use your bank, whether it's withdrawing cash from a machine, paying a bill or ordering a statement, you give them another chance to sell you something. Much in the same way as supermarkets use 'loss leaders' (popular products sold at below cost price in order to attract customers), banks offer banking services – especially current accounts – as a way of attracting and keeping customers.

Don't ever let a bank sell you something that isn't what you need or isn't good value. You should shop for all your financial services in the same way that you shop for anything else. In other words, don't pay more than you have to for your banking.

Loyalty doesn't pay

Don't imagine for a moment that by being loyal to a bank you'll get a better service. Of course, no bank wants to lose its customers, but in most cases if you are unhappy with the service you receive, the threat to take your business elsewhere – unless you are very rich – is unlikely to upset them.

HOW TO FILL IN A CHEQUE

Write the name of the person you want to pay (the 'recipient') here.

Write the amount you want to pay the recipient in words here.

Write the date here.

Write the amount you want to pay the recipient in numerals here.

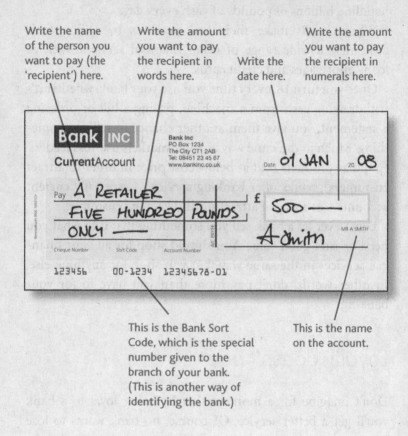

This is the Bank Sort Code, which is the special number given to the branch of your bank. (This is another way of identifying the bank.)

This is the name on the account.

WHAT DOES A CASH CARD LOOK LIKE?

Card number.

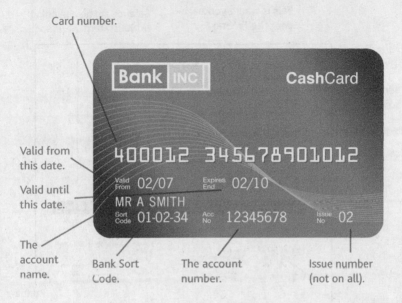

Valid from this date.

Valid until this date.

The account name.

Bank Sort Code.

The account number.

Issue number (not on all).

Security number (last three digits)

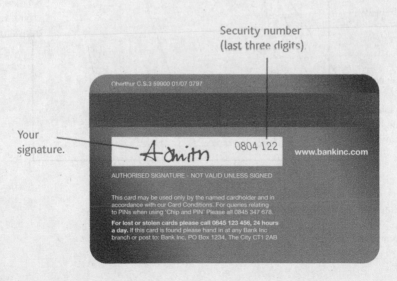

Your signature.

HOW TO READ A BANK STATEMENT

This is where you have deposited money.

Balance at the beginning of the statement period.

Bank branch address.

The address of the account holder.

Bank Sort Code.

The account number.

Date of transaction.

This is a regular payment from your account by direct debit.

This is a regular payment from your account to another account by standing order.

This is where you have taken money out using an ATM.

Type of transaction.

Amount of transaction.

Balance at the end of the statement period.

Running balance after each transaction

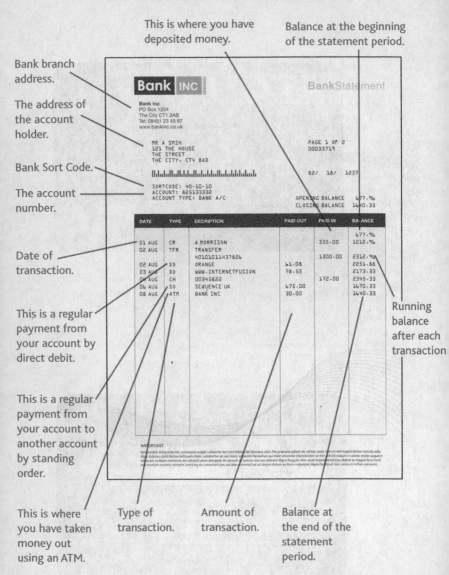

1	Take advantage of free banking for as long as you can – it could be worth as much as £140 a year or more to you.
2	What you want, as soon as possible, is a current account.
3	Building societies are owned by their customers and should offer better service and better value for money.

7 Why plastic isn't that fantastic

After you turn 18, you are likely to start receiving junk mail from banks and other financial institutions inviting you to apply for a credit card.

What these mailings should explain is that a credit card is basically just an overpriced personal loan. Instead, the sales copy always makes a big thing about the status and convenience of having a credit card. You will be flattered and made to feel important. Most of all, you'll be encouraged to imagine all the different ways you could spend the money you are being offered.

Don't be fooled. If you need to borrow money, there are much cheaper ways. Indeed, Matthew Barrett, the former head of Barclays Bank, actually went on record as saying: 'I don't borrow on credit cards, because it is too expensive.' So even the man in charge of one of the biggest credit-card companies in the world, Barclaycard, thinks they offer rotten value.

Not that credit cards are all bad. If you are disciplined and don't let the credit-card companies get the better of you, then you may find having a card useful. But if you want to avoid being ripped off, then you need to be extremely cautious.

Not credit cards, debt cards

A credit card is nothing more than a way of borrowing money. In fact, credit cards really ought to be called 'debt' cards. They work like this:

→ When you receive a credit card, it comes with a 'credit', or spending, limit. This is the amount you are being offered as a loan.

→ Spending your loan is only too easy. Either you can buy goods or services using the card or – if you pay extra – you can take out cash from an ATM or over the counter at a bank.

→ Every month you will receive a statement from the credit-card company telling you how much you have spent and where.

→ When you receive your monthly statement, you can decide to pay off all the money you owe the credit-card company or just part of it.

If you decide to pay off just part of your credit-card balance (and this is what every credit card company wants you to do because they are in the business of lending money), then there will be a minimum payment you must make. This will vary but is usually around 2% of the total debt or £5 – whichever is higher.

How credit cards work

Credit-card companies are set up by banks, building societies and other financial institutions to offer credit cards to their customers. So when we refer to 'credit-card companies' what we actually mean is 'banks'.

As it would be impossible for individual banks to arrange for their credit card to be accepted in millions of outlets all over the world, they employ other firms – like MasterCard and Visa

– to handle most of the administration on their behalf.

Essentially, the banks lend the money and firms like Master-Card and Visa make sure the cardholders have plenty of places to spend it.

Why banks love credit cardholders

Banks charge their customers interest on the money they lend. Usually, they charge much more interest on credit cards than for other types of lending.

For instance, a bank might charge you 6% interest a year if you want to borrow money to buy your own home and 7% interest a year if you want to borrow money to buy, say, a car. But if you want to borrow money on a credit card, the interest charged could be as high as 16% or more a year.

In plain English, for every £1 a bank lends to someone buying his/her own home, it probably makes about 6p a year in interest, BUT for every £1 it lends to a credit cardholder, it could well make 16p or more a year in interest.

So you can see why banks love credit cardholders! Credit-card lending is pretty much the most profitable type of lending possible. Banks earn a fortune from it.

How three months' spending took seven years to repay

When Jack turned 18, his bank wrote and offered him a chance to apply for a credit card, which he did. He was accepted and given a £500 credit limit at an interest rate of 14%. Every month he had to repay a minimum of 2.5% of his total balance or £5 – whichever was greater.

This is what happened over the next three months:

Month 1	Jack spent the following sums on his credit card
Meal out	£22
CDs	£34
Jeans	£26
Railway ticket	£4
Groceries	£19
Total	£105

His minimum payment was £5 but, even after he had made this, he still owed £101.23 due to interest.

Month 2	Jack spent the following sums on his credit card
Trip to cinema	£18
Groceries	£39

Books	£21
Meal out	£24
Total	£102

Jack now owed a total of £203.23. His minimum payment was £5 again but, even after he had paid this, he still owed £200.60 due to interest.

Month 3	Jack spent the following sums on his credit card
Weekend break	£160
Meal out	£12
Shoes	£45
Groceries	£31
Telephone bill	£50
Total	£298

Jack was now up to his £500 limit. His minimum payment was £5.77 but, even after making it, he still owed £499.42 due to interest.

So, in the space of three months, Jack has borrowed £500 which – if he makes the minimum payment of 2.5% every time he gets a statement – would take him seven years to pay off. During this period, he would pay £333.47 in interest.

Cash costs more

You will pay extra interest if you use your credit card to obtain cash (whether from an ATM or in a bank branch) and there is often an extra handling fee. If you have a credit card, you should only use the 'cash advance' facility in a real emergency.

Store cards are even more expensive

Store cards are credit cards you can use in only one particular shop or chain of shops. Shopkeepers have a lot to gain because store-card customers tend to visit more often and spend more money.

In fact, the interest shopkeepers earn on spending made using a store card is often greater than the profit they make from simply selling the goods.

This is because the rates on many of these cards would make a loan shark blush – 25% a year and above is by no means unheard of. No wonder, then, that it is worth the shopkeeper's while to offer you a 10% discount the first time you use the card, invitations to sale previews, interest-free periods and the rest. Once you have a debt of £1,000 on a store card, the shop could be making £250 a year or more from you in interest.

Consider this typical example:

Jane goes shopping in her favourite department store – Miss Flesridge – during the sale and buys £200 worth of clothes at 25% off. Just as she is about to pay the £150, the shop assistant serving her suggests that she takes out a Miss Flesridge Card in order to save an extra 10%. Jane can't resist. So she saves an extra £15 and pays just £135. But instead of paying the whole sum off when she gets her statement, she pays just the minimum amount and carries on doing this. The rate of interest she is being charged is 19%. By the time she finishes paying off the debt, she will have suffered £166 of interest. This is more than the clothes cost her.

When a credit card can make sense

Credit-card debt has become a serious problem in the UK, with growing numbers of people seeking help because they can't afford to make their monthly repayments.

So credit cards are definitely not a good idea for anyone who has an impulsive nature and can't resist the temptation of spending money he/she hasn't really got.

If, however, you have iron discipline and won't be tempted to borrow unnecessarily, then credit cards do offer some benefits:

→ You can delay paying for things for up to six weeks without it costing you anything. This is because there is a gap of between two and six weeks between when you spend money on your card and when you have to pay back the credit-card company. If you time it correctly, therefore, you can get a six-week interest-free loan.
→ Many cards offer free insurance. This can include 'get it home' cover, which means if something you have bought using your credit card gets lost or stolen before you get it home, you can claim back the cost. It may also include some travel insurance.

→ You can use your credit card to reserve things like travel tickets and hotel rooms.

→ A credit card may be the most convenient way to pay when you travel overseas – but check for charges.

If in doubt, just say no

The big risk with a credit card is that you will run up large debts which you have no way of paying off. If you need to borrow money, there are much cheaper ways to do it. And if you don't want to carry cash when you go shopping, use a debit card. Don't let the banks fool you into taking a credit card out. Unless you have a real need, just say no.

A TYPICAL CREDIT CARD

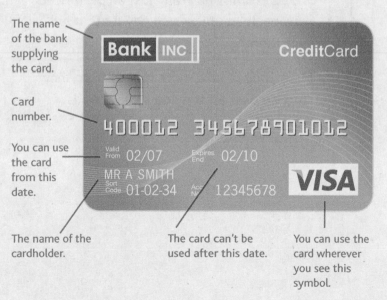

The name of the bank supplying the card.

Card number.

You can use the card from this date.

The name of the cardholder.

The card can't be used after this date.

You can use the card wherever you see this symbol.

You must sign the card here.

Sometimes you will be asked to provide the last three digits of this number here for extra security.

1	A credit card is basically just an overpriced personal loan unless you pay it off in full each month.
2	Many shops make more money from their store cards than they do selling goods.

8 Don't become a loan ranger

Sooner or later – and probably sooner if you want to carry on studying full time after you leave school or need to make a major purchase like a car – you will think about borrowing money.

It goes without saying that it is better not to borrow if you can avoid it. But there are times when you may not be able to avoid it and even times when borrowing does make sense.

If you are going to borrow, keep the following in mind:

→ Don't borrow more than you have to.
→ Pay it back as quickly as you can.
→ Make sure you take out the cheapest possible loan.

If there is one area of personal finance where consumers regularly get ripped off, it is that of borrowing. The easy way to make sure you don't join them is to spend a few minutes reading this chapter.

It pays to shop around

Would you pay £30 for a CD if you could buy exactly the same thing in the shop next door for £10? Or £75 for a pair of jeans if you could buy exactly the same pair in the shop next door for £25?

I doubt it. But, believe it or not, there are people who pay up to THREE times as much interest to borrow money as they have to. Nothing proves this better than a quick comparison of some typical rates:

Personal loan (secured)	7%
Personal loan (unsecured)	8%
Credit card	15%
Store card	25%

Remember, financial institutions make enormous profits from lending money. You should never, ever be shy about shopping around or asking for a lower rate. You could save yourself a small fortune.

How to compare loan rates

So that it is easy for people to compare the cost of different loans, the government says that interest rates must all be shown in terms of an 'annual percentage rate', or 'APR'.

Confusingly, there is more than one way to calculate the APR – but broadly speaking it is an accurate way of assessing how much a loan is going to cost you including all the hidden costs such as upfront fees.

Clearly, the lower the APR, the cheaper the loan and the better it is for you.

When you borrow, you are kissing goodbye to 'future' income

When you borrow, what you are doing is giving away some or all of your future income. Let's say you borrow £250 at 12%

interest and repay it over 36 months. What you are giving the lender is £9.44 of your monthly income for the next three years. What you are paying for this privilege is a grand total of £90 in interest.

The sooner you pay a loan back, the more money you will save

Keeping with the example above, if you borrow £250 and pay it back in six months instead of three years, you save £75 in interest. If you want to save money on your borrowing, it is important not just to shop around for the best rate but also to pay back your loan as quickly as possible.

Sometimes borrowing does make sense

There are times when it may make excellent sense to borrow, for instance:

→ to pay for education
→ to pay for a car or other necessary item
→ to start a business
→ to buy, build or improve your home.

There are also times when it may be difficult to avoid borrowing money – if you are temporarily unable to earn an income, for example, for some reason beyond your control.

There is no real harm, either, in genuine short-term borrowing for a luxury item. What is really dangerous, however, is short-term borrowing that becomes long-term borrowing. For example, buying weekly groceries on a credit card and then not paying the total off immediately. If you only borrow for things that will last longer than it will take you to repay the loan, you can avoid this problem.

How loan rates are set

When you borrow money, you will usually pay a 'variable' rate of interest. This means that the interest rate will rise and fall with the rest of the market. The market itself will be strongly influenced by something called the 'base' rate. This is set by the Bank of England and is – broadly speaking – the rate at which it will lend money to other financial institutions. The base rate can change several times a year, resulting in changes to the interest you may be charged.

If you borrow money at a variable rate, remember that your repayments may go up (or down) until you repay the loan.

It is sometimes possible to take out loans on a 'fixed' rate of interest. This means that the rate of interest you pay – and your repayments – will always be the same while you have the loan in place.

DON'T BECOME A LOAN RANGER

Choose the best loan for your needs

Here is a quick summary of the loan options available to you until you have security (such as a home of your own) to offer to lenders. For student loans see Chapter 11. Remember, by law, banks and financial institutions aren't allowed to lend you money until after your 18th birthday.

Loans from family, friends and employers

Often family members, friends and employers will make interest-free or low-interest loans. It is best to have a written agreement so that there is no room for misunderstanding or bad feeling at a later date.

Overdrafts

If you have a bank current account, you can ask your manager for an authorised overdraft facility. See Chapter 6 for details.

Personal or term loans

The cost of personal or term loans can vary enormously. Essentially, when you borrow the money, you agree to a set repayment period, or 'term'. For example, you might agree to pay the money back in 36 monthly payments.

Dealer and shop loans

Where a loan is provided by a dealer (like a car dealer, for instance) or through a shop, check the small print closely. Sometimes you may be offered a low or zero rate of interest for an agreed period that will rise dramatically in cost after the set term. Remember, the cost of providing this sort of loan will be built into the price of whatever you are buying. Shop around!

106

Hire purchase

Hire purchase allows you to buy specific goods over an agreed period of time. In other words, it is a bit like a personal or term loan. The difference is that the rates charged for hire purchase are normally somewhat higher and you might be better looking at alternatives, such as a personal loan. Remember, too, that with hire purchase you don't own whatever you are buying until you have made your last payment. This is not usually the case with, say, a personal loan.

Credit cards

Credit cards are an extremely expensive way to borrow, and credit-card companies are very aggressive in their marketing methods. If you are going to use a credit card, then don't fall into the trap of making the minimum payment each month. A relatively small balance could take you years to clear.

Store cards

These work in the same way as credit cards except, of course, you can only use them in the store (or chain of stores) that issues the card. Their single advantage is that having such a card may entitle you to benefits, such as an extra discount on first purchase and again during any sales. Their huge disadvantage is that the rate of interest charged on outstanding balances almost always makes normal credit cards look cheap by comparison. My strong advice – unless you are very disciplined with money – is not to use store cards.

Pawnbrokers

A bank won't accept something small and second-hand as security – such as a watch or clothes – but a pawnbroker will.

'Pawning' (the process of borrowing money against one or more of your possessions) is expensive, as the rate of interest is normally set quite high. What's more, if you don't repay the agreed amount before the day specified, you lose whatever you have pawned.

Moneylenders

Whether licensed or unlicensed, moneylenders are almost always the most expensive way to borrow and the rates they charge are outrageous. When they are trading illegally, there is the added risk of violence or intimidation if you don't pay what they say you owe them. You should avoid them like the plague!

A cheaper way to borrow when you are a bit older

When you are a bit older and own your own home or other valuable assets, you may well be able to cut the cost of your borrowing by taking out a 'secured' loan. A secured loan is one where the lender has 'security' – almost always property – that can be sold to repay the loan if the borrower stops his or her payments for any reason.

Lenders don't like selling a property in order to get their money back. They will often wait months, even years, before taking such drastic action. Still, it gives them peace of mind and this in turn means that borrowers benefit from much lower interest charges.

How some lenders trick their customers

As you may have gathered, I am not a big fan of the way in which many banks and other lenders treat their borrowers. Of course, there are some ethical lenders who are careful not to lend money to people who can't afford to pay it back. And there are lenders who aren't greedy when it comes to charging interest. On the whole, however, I have a low opinion of lenders.

One of the reasons I know so much about the subject is that for many years my job was to write junk mail and sales copy for banks, building societies and other financial institutions. I am sorry I did it now! Anyway, the least I can do is let you know exactly how lenders set out to confuse and trick their customers.

Don't get caught in the minimum-payment trap

Lenders want you to repay them. Wrong. The last thing most lenders want is for you to pay back the money you owe them. Why would they, when they can make massive profits at your expense? This is why lenders frequently set very low minimum monthly payments. By making sure that most of what you repay them is interest (and not the debt itself), they can prolong the agony for you and increase the profits for themselves. Nothing makes lenders so happy as a customer who falls into the minimum-payment trap.

The lure of revolving credit

Keeping you in debt for the longest possible period is only one of the objectives every lender has. Their other main objective is to encourage you to borrow as much money as possible. The easiest way for them to do this is to keep offering you bigger and bigger loans. This practice is referred to as 'revolving credit'.

The variable cost of borrowing

Lenders have one other powerful weapon with which to maximise their profits: the rate of interest they charge. At the moment we are in what is referred to as a 'low interest-rate environment'. Yet, despite this fact, many lenders charge extortionate rates of interest. It is not uncommon, for instance, for credit-card companies to charge 16% a year or more.

How lenders keep the true cost of borrowing from their customers

Another dodgy thing lenders do is not make it crystal clear

to their customers how much a loan is going to cost. They do this in a number of ways:

→ Not writing the contract in plain English, making it impossible for anyone who isn't a solicitor to understand it. Have you ever tried to read a loan agreement? It isn't easy.
→ Small print. When it isn't printed so small that you can barely read it, it is printed in an illegible typeface with the words squeezed close together.
→ Quoting low, so-called 'easy', monthly payments to make it sound as if the loan is cheap.
→ Not stating upfront and in large print exactly how much interest you are going to pay.
→ Hidden charges and fees.
→ Holding out the promise of one interest rate ('from 9% a year') but then charging you much, much more.

Of all the things that lenders do to fool their customers, the one that irritates me most is the habit of not saying upfront and in large print what your loan is going to cost in cash terms.

For example, when you buy a car for £10,000 over five years using 'dealer finance', it should be emphasised that once interest has been added (let's take a typical rate of 12% a year) the car is actually going to cost you around £16,000.

The wily use of so-called reward schemes, special offers and deals

As the competition to lend money has increased, banks have come up with all sorts of incentives to encourage consumers to borrow more. Incentives that, on the face of it, seem to be in your favour, such as:

→ 0% interest for a period of time
→ a low rate of interest for a period of time
→ a fixed rate of interest for a period of time
→ reward schemes giving you free gifts if you borrow more money
→ cashback when you take out the loan.

In fact, all of these incentives actually work in the lender's favour. For instance, many of the customers who take advantage of interest 'deals' (0% finance and the like) invariably pay extra charges and/or end up switching to a high rate of interest at the end of the term. Reward schemes – such as Air Miles – cost the lenders very little and they factor this into the interest rates they charge, while it is you – the customer – who picks up the cost of any cash you get handed back.

Remember, nothing is 'free' in life. Lenders aren't fools: if they offer you something, you can be certain it is more than worth their while to do so.

The language lenders use to make you feel special

Lenders use language to great effect to make borrowers borrow more. To begin with, they flatter their customers by telling them that they have been 'specially selected' or are in some other way honoured to be offered a particular loan. Then they play down the expense of the loan with expressions such as 'low cost' and 'value for money'. Finally, they focus not on the interest rate or term but on the monthly payments, which they will describe as being 'easy' and 'convenient'.

1	Believe it or not, there are people who pay THREE times as much interest to borrow money than they have to.
2	When you borrow, what you are doing is giving away some or all of your future income.
3	The last thing a lender wants is for you to pay back the money you owe.

9 How to turn £1 a day into £118,025

There are lots of ways in which you could end up with plenty of cash to do what you want with.

You might win the lottery, for instance, or unexpectedly inherit a fortune or uncover a treasure trove.

But if you want to guarantee yourself a nice, fat bank balance, then there is only one thing to do: save.

Put away a little money on a regular basis and you will be amazed how quickly it grows.

A writer called F. Scott Fitzgerald once remarked: 'The rich are different', to which another writer, Ernest Hemingway, replied: 'Yes, they have more money.' This chapter is about how you can have more money; in fact, it is about how you can become rich, simply by saving. As Sophie Tucker, a singer, observed: 'I've been rich, and I've been poor; rich is better.'

Set your savings goals

Perhaps the best thing about having money is the freedom it brings. With cash in the bank you can do what you want, when you want to do it, without having to rely on anyone else.

The first step to building up some savings is to set yourself goals. For instance, you might like to have money tucked away in order to:

→ ensure that you are never stuck for cash in an emergency
→ pay for something specific, such as a holiday, computer or your living expenses while studying
→ help you start building up some serious wealth.

You may have a specific target. For instance, you might want

£500 to buy a new computer in three months' time. Or you could just want the luxury of having money available to spend as you like. Either way, the sensible thing to do is divide your savings up:

→ Keep some where you can get your hands on it quickly.
→ Put the rest where it may not be as easy to get hold of but where you should earn much bigger profits.

There are plenty of different savings and investment options that will allow you to do this.

Get the savings habit

Saving comes naturally to some people, and is extremely difficult for others. Like any skill, the best way to learn it is to practise. Most money experts recommend saving part of any money you receive. For instance, if you earn £30 a week, you might save £10 a week, or, if you get given £50 for your birthday, you might save £25 of it.

Remember, thanks to compound interest, if you leave your savings to grow over the longer term, you can make yourself very wealthy.

The chart below shows what saving different amounts of money every day might earn you if you started at 18 and stopped at different ages between 40 and 60.

As you can see, just £1 a day could become £118,025 by the time you reach 60 and **£10 a day could become a staggering £1,180,253!**

	At 40	At 50	At 60
£1 a day would be worth	£21,513	£52,066	£118,025
£2 a day would be worth	£43,027	£104,131	£236,051
£5 a day would be worth	£107,567	£260,328	£590,127
£10 a day would be worth	£215,134	£520,655	£1,180,253

Make sure you don't pay tax on your savings

The interest you receive from savings and investments is taxed – usually before it is handed over to you.

However, if you are under 18, you will almost certainly be able to receive interest without having to pay this tax.

Every time you open an account that pays interest you should complete a special government form called *R85*. This will be given to you by your bank or building society. If you are under 16, you will have to get a parent or guardian to complete and sign the form for you. Once you have completed it, you won't have to pay tax on any interest.

Even if you are over 18, it is possible for you to save money without paying tax by choosing a tax-free account.

Choose the best home for your money

You will find that all the different savings and investment options can be divided into:

→ easy-to-access homes for your money that probably won't make you much profit
→ homes for your money that make it harder to get hold of but that should, in theory, make you much bigger profits.

Right now we are going to look at the easy-to-access homes for your money – which is what you should start with. If you are interested in building your wealth over the longer term (years as opposed to months), then you should turn to Chapter 15.

Remember, it pays to shop around. While researching this book, I found one deposit account that paid just 1% a year in interest and another that paid 10%! If you had saved, say, £200 in the '1%' account, you would have made £2 in interest. Whereas, if you had saved £200 in the '10%' account, you would have made £20 in interest.

Deposit accounts

If you leave money on 'deposit' with a bank or building society, they will pay you interest. How much interest you earn will vary according to:

→ how much money you have on deposit
→ the amount of warning (referred to as 'notice') you have to give before you can make a withdrawal (take some or all of your money out).

119

How do you make sure you are getting the best rate of interest? There is a website called Moneyfacts (www.moneyfacts.co.uk) which will tell you which bank or building society is offering the best return. Here are a few tips to help you get the most from a deposit account:

→ Youth and children's accounts tend to pay higher interest rates and offer all sorts of freebies like CDs and money-off vouchers.
→ If you open an account online with a bank or building society, you will often get a better interest rate.
→ Don't hesitate to move your money to where the best deal is to be had.
→ If you are willing to wait before you can get your hands on your money, you will earn much more interest.
→ Read the small print! Some banks may give you less interest than they promise if you don't meet all their conditions.

What features should you look for in a deposit account? The most important feature is the rate of interest.

Premium Bonds
A good alternative to a deposit account is to buy Premium Bonds. Every Bond you buy gives you a chance to win one of thousands of cash prizes each month for as long as you keep them. The biggest prizes are worth £1 million each. Although you don't earn interest from a Premium Bond, if you hold onto them over the long term, you should win prizes that add up to roughly the same as a 3% return. The minimum investment is £100 and all the winnings are tax-free. Premium Bonds are offered by the government and you can cash them in at any

time. You'll find a leaflet and application form for Premium Bonds in your local post office or visit the National Savings & Investments website at www.nsandi.com.

Individual Savings Accounts

If you are 16 or over and unable to claim your interest tax-free, you could consider opening an ISA, or Individual Savings Account. You can save up to a certain amount in an ISA each year and not pay a penny of tax on any interest you make. Some ISAs give you instant access to your money – but you should be aware that if you take money out and put it back in again the account may lose its tax-free status.

What is AER?

Nowadays, bank and building society deposit account interest rates are usually followed by the initials AER in brackets like this: 5.8% (AER). In plain English the AER (Annual Equivalent Rate) is the amount of interest you will receive if it is compounded and added to your account once a year.

1	With cash in the bank you can do what you want, when you want to do it.
2	If you want to guarantee yourself a nice, fat bank balance, then there is only one thing to do: get the saving habit.

10 Have money, will travel

VH-30947

If you are heading overseas – whether it is for a quick European break or a longer trip further afield – one of the most important things to organise is your money.

There are three different things you need to think about:

1. Making sure your money is safe and that if it is lost or stolen you won't be badly out of pocket.
2. Making sure you have easy access to your money.
3. Making sure you don't pay a penny more than you have to in commission and other charges.

Spending money abroad can be surprisingly expensive. Get it wrong and you could be paying as much as 10p in fees or commission for every £1 you spend. Which is why, before you travel, it will be well worth your while to read what follows.

How currency works

As you are probably aware, every country in the world has its own money – or currency – with the exception of the 13 countries comprising the Eurozone, which share a single currency called the euro.

When you travel to a particular country, everything you buy will be priced in that country's national currency. For instance, if you go to the United States, you will have to pay in American dollars (US$). Therefore, to spend money, you will have to buy American dollars using your British pounds (UK£), which is called 'exchanging' your money (hence the term 'currency exchange').

At the time of writing this book, UK£1 will buy you

roughly US$2. I say 'roughly' because:

→ currency exchange rates go up and down all the time
→ banks and other organisations that buy and sell currency don't all use the same exchange rate
→ banks and other organisations that buy and sell currency all charge different commission levels and fees.

In fact, the difference between buying foreign currency from one bank as opposed to another might be as much as 5%. Losing 5% on changing your money may not sound that bad, but it means you lose an extra 5p for every pound you spend. Which is why it makes sense to shop around and check rates.

Incidentally, I said that you must always spend money using the national currency of whatever country you are visiting. This isn't strictly true. In countries with weak economies, local traders will be very keen to get their hands on a 'hard' currency, such as British pounds, American dollars or European euros. Such traders may refuse to accept the local currency.

Four basic options

There are four ways to take and spend your money abroad.

The first is with travellers' cheques. These special cheques offer you all the benefits of having cash (you can spend them pretty much anywhere or swap them for the currency of your choice) with the added advantage that if they ever get lost or stolen you will receive all your money back, usually within a matter of hours. As you can imagine, the security with travellers' cheques is pretty tight: each one is numbered, you sign them once when you buy them and once again when you use them and they are only valid if you show your passport. You can buy them in British pounds, American dollars or European euros and you can cash any that are left over when you get back home without trouble.

The second is to use credit cards. If you have a MasterCard or Visa card, you will find that you can pay for pretty much anything, anywhere in the world. You can also take out cash from ATMs and over the counter at banks. If your card is lost or stolen, your bank will replace it (usually within a day), and under normal circumstances it won't cost you anything extra.

Thirdly, you can use your normal cash card. Nowadays, most British ATM cards are recognised by ATMs in other countries. So from Paris in France to Perth in Australia you can take money directly out of your normal bank account via an ATM machine. However, if you lose your cash card overseas, you may find that your bank refuses to replace it until you get back home.

Finally, you can take cash either in local currency or in British pounds. Obviously, if this gets lost or stolen, you won't be able to claim it back from anyone (though some travel insurance policies do offer a certain amount of cover).

Which option is right for you?

How you should arrange your money depends very much on where you are going and how long you will be away. If you are going for more than a day or two, you should probably aim to use a combination of all four options:

1. Travellers' cheques for most of your money because it is safest.
2. A credit card in case of an emergency or for convenience when making major purchases.
3. An ATM card if you need more cash unexpectedly.
4. A small amount of cash so that you can pay for things the moment you arrive.

Going abroad? Don't forget to take out travel insurance

You don't want anything to spoil your holiday or trip abroad. Imagine, for example, how awful it would be if your travel company suddenly closed down, you were involved in an accident or your luggage was lost or stolen. To protect yourself against the financial cost of anything bad happening before or during your holiday (including having to cancel because you are ill), you should take out travel insurance. You will find there is a big difference in price, so shop around. Look out, too, for special deals for students.

The cost of travel money

You need to be very mindful of the costs associated with taking money abroad, because they can quickly add up. Here are a few useful tips:

→ It is often possible to buy travellers' cheques for little or no commission via your bank or building society. It may even be worth opening a special account somewhere in order to get commission-free travellers' cheques. This can be a big saving as otherwise you could easily pay 1% or more when you buy the cheques.

→ When you come to cash in your travellers' cheques or pay for something, double-check the rate of exchange you are being offered. It is well worth shopping around.

→ If you use a credit card abroad, it is almost impossible to know what rate of exchange you will be obliged to pay, as it is set by the credit-card company each day. Also, you may be charged an extra sum and interest when you use the card abroad. Plus, and this is really something to avoid, if you take cash out using your credit card, you can expect to pay all sorts of extra fees.

→ Using your cash card can be very cost-effective if you have an account with a bank or building society that charges little or nothing for the privilege. You should check this before you leave home, as some banks will hit you with all sorts of extra fees.

It pays to shop around

As with everything, it will pay for you to shop around. With a bit of careful planning you can probably get the cost of spending money abroad down to 2% or less of the total amount you use.

THE 13 COUNTRIES THAT NOW USE THE EURO AS THEIR NATIONAL CURRENCY

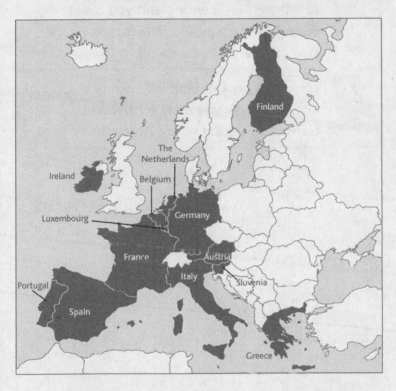

Austria, Belgium, Finland, France, Germany, Greece, Ireland, Italy, Luxembourg, the Netherlands, Portugal, Slovenia and Spain all use one currency – the euro. Like the American dollar, the euro is widely accepted in many other countries, even though it is not legal tender.

1	Spending money abroad can be surprisingly expensive. Get it wrong and you could be paying as much as 10p in fees or commission for every £1 you spend.
2	Look for a bank or building society that doesn't charge you at all for overseas transactions using your cash card.

11 Money for students

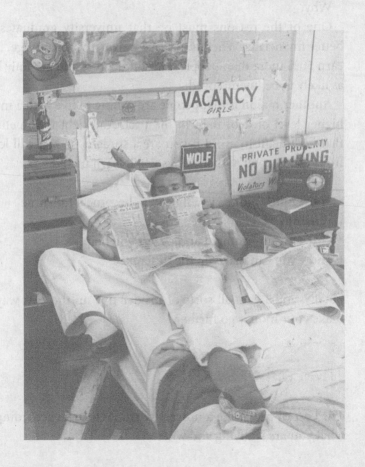

It used to be that school leavers hoping to go to university only had to worry about getting the right exam results.

Nowadays, however, they face another problem: how to pay for their studies – because as the cost of being a full-time student has gone up and up, so the available government support has come down and down.

Despite this, more school leavers are enrolling at university than ever before.

Why?

One of the reasons must be that university graduates do better financially. When they leave university, on average, they earn 50% more than people without degrees and are only half as likely to be unemployed.

Another reason is that people are willing to live with a much higher level of debt than in the past. And debt is something that is difficult to avoid if you are a student, as you will learn from this chapter. Other things you'll learn include:

→ how much money you'll need to become a full-time student
→ how the government and others will help
→ how you can make up the difference.

Finally, you'll gain all sorts of insider tips on the best way to make your money go further.

The cost of studying

The cost of becoming a university student varies according to what you are studying and where.

If you aren't living at home, you are likely to need about £10,000 a year if studying in London and about £8,500 if studying in some other part of the country. This, by the way, is just for the 39-week academic year and doesn't include any money for the holidays. What students may need and what they actually get are, of course, two very different matters. A government survey found that on average students are spending about £7,000 a year. How does this break down? If you go to university, you can expect three different types of expense:

1. Housing. This is by far the biggest expense, with most students spending over half their money on somewhere to live.
2. Living expenses. These include not just the cost of food, household goods, personal spending and entertainment but also travel.
3. Educational expenses. These include tuition fees, books, stationery and other related costs.

Before we look at what money is available to help you meet these costs (and how to find the rest), it is worth considering these expenses in more detail.

The cost of housing

Most universities offer their first-year students an opportunity to live in halls of residence. The average cost of living in halls is about £90 a week including two meals a day, and about £60 a week without food. This said, the cheapest hall of residence in the UK costs about £40 a week and the most expensive £250 a week – so there is huge variation.

Assuming that you don't live in hall and can't live at home for free, you will have to find somewhere to rent. Unless you have a private income or wealthy parents willing to support you, the chances are that this will mean sharing a flat or house and possibly sharing a bedroom. Outside London this is likely to cost you a little over £60 a week, and in London close to £80 a week. When looking for private accommodation, remember that on top of rent you may have to pay a share of the utility bills (heat, water, electricity and so forth). Don't forget, either, that you will have to budget for getting to and from college for lectures.

One final thing to bear in mind is council tax. Most full-time students, but not all, are exempt. You certainly won't have to pay it if you are in hall. But you may be asked for it in private, rented accommodation. If you are having problems, ask your university welfare officer for help.

The cost of living

The second major cost for you as a student – again, assuming you aren't living at home for free or in hall – is that of living expenses and, in particular, food.

On average, students spend around £40 a week on food, £30 a week on socialising and entertainment and close to £15 a week on mobile phone calls. Those who can afford it may also spend money on clothes and other luxury items, such as music and eating out.

Educational expenses

In order to meet their costs, universities charge annual fees of up to £3,070. In addition you will have to find money to pay for books (on average £75 per term), course equipment (on average £57 a term), photocopying and stationery (on average £10 a term) and Internet access (on average £35 a term).

Finding the money to pay for university

There are a number of different ways to pay for university. You can:

→ borrow money from the government
→ apply for grants, bursaries and scholarships
→ borrow money from family or friends
→ borrow money from a bank or building society
→ work in your spare time
→ ask family or friends to give you money
→ find private individuals or a company willing to sponsor your studies.

Borrowing money from the government

The government will lend you money to help with the cost of your fees and living expenses (maintenance) while you are at university. How much you can borrow will depend on where you are studying and whether or not you live at home.

→ You can apply for a loan to cover the full cost of student fees regardless of your personal circumstances.

→ The most you can borrow to pay your living expenses is £3,495 a year if you live at home, £4,510 if you live away from home outside London and £6,315 if you live away from home in London.

You won't be expected to start repaying your student loan until you are earning a minimum of £15,000 a year. After that, you will only be expected to make relatively small monthly payments. For instance, someone earning £18,000 a year would have to repay just £5.19 a week. You will pay interest but it is set at the same level as inflation. In real terms this means you will never have to pay back more than you borrow. All the above figures refer to the academic year starting September 2007. If you haven't repaid your student loan within 25 years, under current rules you never have to pay it.

Applying for grants, bursaries and scholarships

Around half of all full-time students should also be able to claim either a maintenance grant or a special support grant of up to £2,765 a year (from September 2007). This money does not have to be paid back. You may also be eligible for grants, bursaries and scholarships from your university and from your local authority.

If you have to borrow elsewhere

If you are forced to borrow money over and above what you receive under the government Student Loan Scheme, then it will pay you to keep your interest costs to a minimum. Many banks and building societies offer students interest-free or low-interest loans, and these will offer better value than ordinary loans and especially credit cards. Shop around and don't hesitate to move your borrowing to where it will cost you the least. Once you go into debt, it can be tempting to think that borrowing a little extra won't matter. But every extra penny you borrow will delay the day when all your future earnings are yours to spend as you want.

Don't panic

The thought of having to borrow a large amount of money – even if much of it is from the government – to pay for your studies may upset you. But you shouldn't panic. Remember two important things. First of all, you are not alone. The vast majority of students are in the same position. Secondly, once you finish university, you can immediately look forward to a much, much higher income than someone without a degree.

Making your money go further

When money is tight, one of the best ways to make it go further is to budget. We looked at budgeting in Chapter 5, so there's no need to go over the theory of it again. But you may find it helpful to use this checklist to draw up a weekly budget for when you are studying.

Income
→ Government grant towards fees
→ University bursary towards fees
→ Student loan
→ Loan from family or friends
→ Bank/building society loan

→ Job (term time)
→ Job (holidays)
→ Grants
→ Bursaries
→ Scholarships
→ Gifts
→ Sponsorship

Spending

→ University fees
→ Books
→ Course equipment
→ Course trips
→ Stationery
→ Photocopying
→ Internet
→ Travel including to and from lectures
→ Rent
→ Electricity
→ Gas
→ Telephone
→ TV licence
→ Food
→ Eating out
→ Laundry
→ Cosmetics and toiletries
→ Entertainment
→ Drinking
→ Club memberships
→ Clothes
→ Music, books and magazines

→ Gifts
→ Driving lessons
→ Holidays

Should you take out 'student insurance'?

If you won't be living at home during your time at university, you should consider taking out some special 'student insurance' to protect your possessions. Then, if anything of yours – such as your computer, stereo, clothes, books and so forth – gets lost, stolen or damaged, you won't have to pay for replacing it yourself. There are several companies offering this type of insurance – to find them try an online search engine such as Google and request 'student insurance UK'. Or ask your university welfare office for recommendations. It may also be worth contacting your parents' insurance company, as some firms will provide student cover for free or for a small additional charge.

More information

The best way to find out what you are entitled to is to visit the government's main information website at www.direct.gov.uk.

Another useful source of information is the Department for Children, Schools and Families. Telephone: 0870 000 2288; website: www.dfes.gov.uk.

The National Union of Students (NUS) publishes a great deal of relevant information. Telephone: 0871 221 8221; website: www.nusonline.co.uk.

Every year Trotman & Company publishes a book entitled *Students' Money Matters* by Gwenda Thomas that contains a great deal of detailed advice and a useful 'frequently asked questions' section. If you don't want to buy a copy, try your local library.

Finally, your school, chosen university and local authority should all be able to provide additional help and information.

1	It pays to go to university. Graduates earn 50% more than people without degrees and are only half as likely to be unemployed.
2	A student loan from the government is one of the cheapest ways to borrow.

12 Work, tax and benefits

Whenever you plan to start work, whether it is full or part time, it is important to know about:

→ your rights
→ how to read a payslip
→ tax
→ your entitlement to state benefits.

Your rights

When you go to work for someone, you are protected by law against your boss:

→ making you do something dangerous
→ making you work for too long at any one time
→ taking financial advantage of you
→ not paying you properly.

If you are in a permanent job, you may be given a special 'employment contract' with extra rights. Your employer can't, however, ever take away rights that are yours by law.

Before you turn 16

Your local authority is in charge of making sure that young people and children under the age of 16 are not exploited. The rules can be slightly different from area to area, but in general:

→ You are not allowed to do any work at all until you are 10, at which point you are allowed to do odd jobs for your parents such as gardening (the only exception to this is for children involved in television, theatre or similar activities).

→ Between the ages of 13 and 16 you are only allowed to do part-time work, outside school hours, that doesn't interfere with your schoolwork (there are all sorts of jobs you cannot do and there are strict limits on the hours you can work).

→ You are not allowed to work without an employment permit – but you don't need one if you are working for your parents, doing work that is not for profit, including helping a charity or babysitting, or undertaking work experience arranged by your school. The education department of your local council issues permits and it is the responsibility of your boss to make the arrangements.

To find out what your rights are, visit the government information website at www.direct.gov.uk and search for 'children's rights' or contact your local council.

Between the ages of 16 and 18

Between the ages of 16 and 18 you are treated almost the same as an adult worker. This means you are entitled to all sorts of benefits, such as holiday pay, sick pay and redundancy pay. You cannot be made to work for the same number of hours, though, and you must receive extra breaks.

Once you turn 16, you can apply for a National Insurance number. You should do this if you need to claim state benefits (in which case your local Jobcentre Plus office will help you), if you get a job or if you start working for yourself (in which case call 0845 600 0643 during working hours). National Insurance is handled by the Department for Work and Pensions – you'll find their telephone number in the phone book or visit their website at www.dwp.gov.uk.

To learn about your rights visit the government information website at www.direct.gov.uk and search for 'employment legislation' and 'working time regulations'.

Minimum wage

Once you turn 16, you are covered by the national minimum wage law. This law is supposed to make sure that no one is paid less than a certain amount per hour. The rates from 1st October 2007 are:

Age	Hourly rate
16, 17	£3.40
18, 19, 20, 21	£4.60
22 or over	£5.52

There are some exceptions to this. To find out what your rights are, visit the government information website at www.direct.gov.uk and search for 'national minimum wage'.

Your tax position

Regardless of your age, once you start earning more than a certain amount of money each year you will have to pay income tax and National Insurance contributions. The amount you have to earn before tax kicks in is called your 'personal allowance' and it is set each year by the government. There are other allowances you may be able to claim, for example if you are married or blind.

Once you start paying tax, the amount you pay is linked to the amount you earn. Here's how it works for 2007–8 if you are single and not entitled to any extra allowances:

On the first £5,225	No tax
On the next £2,230	10% tax
Anything between £7,231 and £34,600	22% tax
Anything over £34,600	40% tax

In other words, you can earn roughly £435 a month and not pay any tax – after which the more you earn, the more you pay.

An example of how income tax works

Nat leaves university and gets a good job earning £20,000 a year. Because he is single and without children, his tax bill for 2007–8 looks like this:

He doesn't pay any tax on the first	£5,225	£0
He pays 10% on the next	£2,230	£223
He pays 22% on the next	£12,545	£2,759
	Total amount earned £20,000	Total tax £2,982

> After tax he is left with £17,018 (£20,000 less £2,982), which divided by 12 (as he is paid monthly) is £1,418 a month. However, as he also has to pay National Insurance – see below – he'll actually receive less than this. Note that the 10% 'starting' rate is due to end in 2008–9 and that the 22% rate is due to drop to 20%.

Here are a few other things you should know about income tax before you start work:

→ Income tax will be taken out of your wages before you receive them. This system is called 'Pay As You Earn' or PAYE. Your employer has to do this by law.

→ The tax year is different from the calendar year. For historic reasons it starts on 6th April one year and ends on 5th April the next.

→ Your employer will spread your personal allowance out over the whole year.

→ At the end of a tax year if you have paid more tax than you actually owed, you will receive a refund.

→ When you start work, you will probably be put on 'emergency tax' until your situation is sorted out. If you pay too much, you'll be entitled to a refund.

National Insurance

There is a second, much smaller tax you will have to pay on your earnings once you have turned 16. It is called National Insurance, or NI (sometimes referred to as National Insurance Contributions, or NIC), and it is important because once you have paid a certain amount of it you are entitled to extra state benefits. For instance, if you want to claim the Jobseeker's Allowance, incapacity benefit (if you become ill) or a state pension, you must have paid NI.

Confusingly, the system is arranged in such a way that sometimes, even though you haven't actually paid any NI, you will be treated as if you have.

You pay NI until you reach the state pension age, which is now 65 for anyone retiring after 2020.

Good news for students

Do you expect to be a student for the whole tax year? Do you only work in the holidays? Do you expect your income (excluding grants, loans and scholarships) to be within the personal allowance – £5,225 for 2007–8? If you can answer 'yes' to these three questions, fill in the student tax exemption form *P38(S)* – available from your local tax office –

to avoid having tax deducted from your wages.

Your tax code

Your employer must, by law, act as a tax collector and take the tax and NI you owe and pay it to the government on your behalf. To make sure that your employer collects the right amount of tax, you will be issued with a tax code. This will be sent to you at the start of the year in a letter with the heading 'Notice of Coding'. Your employer will explain your tax code to you or you can contact your nearest tax office (look in your telephone book under HM Revenue & Customs or visit their website at www.hmrc.gov.uk).

Your payslip

Once you start working on a formal basis for an employer, you will receive a payslip (see diagram below) when (or slightly before) you get paid. The purpose of this payslip is to explain what pay you are receiving and what deductions have been made. If you have any questions, you should speak with your boss or, if there is one, the accounts department. Here are a few tips:

→ Payslips don't all look the same, but by law they must all contain the same information.
→ Your pay after deductions may be given to you in cash,

as a cheque or paid straight into your bank account.
→ Remember, you may be put on emergency tax when you get your first job, which is why the tax element could seem rather large.

A quick guide to tax

Tax is the money the government takes from you to pay for public services such as:

→ schools, colleges and universities
→ roads
→ police
→ hospitals and medical care
→ defending the country
→ helping those who are elderly, ill, disabled or unable to work.

Tax is a political tool. Different governments use it in different ways. For instance, one government might feel that rich people should pay more tax than poor people in order to make society a fairer place. Another government might feel that the state should be less involved in people's lives and that tax rates should be lower.

Tax also offers governments a way to:

→ discourage certain behaviour, for example taxing cigarettes to try to stop people from smoking so much
→ encourage certain behaviour, for example you pay less tax when you save money for your old age.

A PAYSLIP

Your name

Employee number: If you work for a large employer, you will be given a number to make it easier to identify you.

Tax code: This tells your employer how much tax to take out of your pay.

N.I. Number: Th is your National Insurance numb

Pensionable salary: This is the total yearly salary you receive.

Overtime: This is any money you have earned for over-time during the period shown.

Bonus/other pay: This is any other amount you are being paid. For instance, a Christmas bonus.

Name: Mr AN EMPLOYEE		Pay date: 29/09/2008	
Employee No: 1094804		Tax period: 06	
		Tax Code: 16L 1	

Pensionable Salary:	35000	N.I. Number: XF648088C
Basic Hrs per Week:	35.00	N.I. Code: D
Hourly rate:	19.2307	
Overtime:	0.00	
Bonus/Other:	0.00	

PAYMENTS	£pp	DEDUCTIONS	£pp
SALARY	2916.66	Income Tax:	761.40
		National Ins:	145.27
		Pension Cont.	133.27
TOTAL PAYMENTS	2916.66	TOTAL DEDUCTIONS	939.94

Gross pay: This is the total amount your employer owes you for the period being shown (usually one week, two weeks or – in this case – a month), before any tax or other deductions are made.

Tax this period: This is the amount of income tax that you have to pay to the government for this tax period. It will be deducted from your gross salary.

National Insurance: This is the amount of National Insurance you have to pay to the government for this pay period. It will be deducted from your gross salary.

Tax period: This is the period covered by the pay slip. It is usually shown as a number. If you are paid weekly, then the numbers will run from 1 to 52, but if you are paid monthly, they will run from 1 to 12. Because tax has a special year (6th April one year to 5th April the next), the first pay period will start in early April.

YEAR TO DATE	£pp
Taxable Payments:	17515.98
Emp. Pension Cont:	799.62
Taxable Pay:	16716.36
Tax:	3984.80
NIC Employee:	871.80
NIC Employer:	1479.36
PAYMENT METHODS AND ACCOUNT DETAILS	
B.A.C.S.	1979.39
Sort Code: 653234	
Account No.: 19393850	
NET PAY	1979.39

Employer NIC: This is the amount of National Insurance your employer has to pay to the government on your behalf. This costs you nothing. Your employer has to pay this by law. In this case the amount shown is the total that the employer has paid on the employee's behalf since the start of the tax year

Net pay: This is what you have left!

Total deductions: This is the total of everything you have had deducted from your salary – tax, NI and so forth.

Pension deduction: If you are in a pension scheme, this is the money that has been taken out of your salary and paid towards your pension.

It is tax that allows us to live in a safe, well-ordered society where everyone has plenty of opportunity and the less fortunate are looked after. You may hate having to pay it, but at least it is going towards a good cause.

The business of saving tax

Whether or not you have to pay tax (and how much you have to pay) is strictly controlled by law. If you don't pay what you owe, you could be fined and even sent to prison. However, it is perfectly legal to use our tax laws in any way you can to reduce the amount of tax you pay.

**Illegal tax saving is called 'tax evasion'.
Legal tax saving is called 'tax avoidance'.**

Because there are so many rules, it is often possible to find reasons not to pay as much tax. This is called finding a 'tax loophole'.

There are lots of other reasons why you might not have to pay so much tax. For instance, if you:

→ have spent money on things connected with your work, for example if you are a plumber and buy some tools
→ have a family or someone else to support
→ are saving money for when you retire
→ aren't earning much money
→ have a clever accountant!

Know your enemy!

Here is a brief description of the main UK taxes.

Income tax

This is a tax on your annual income (the money you earn every year). How much you have to pay is linked to how much you earn and your personal circumstances. For instance, if you are single, you will probably pay more than if you are married.

National Insurance

If you are employed or self-employed (you work for yourself), you pay National Insurance. This goes towards paying for things like pensions when you are old.

Value added tax (VAT)

This is a tax on your spending. It is charged at different rates from 0% to 17.5%, depending on what you are buying. Quite a few basics (everything from food to nappies, and from books to children's clothes) don't have VAT added to them. But most things do.

Capital gains tax

If you buy something at one price and then sell it later for a higher price, then you will have made a 'capital gain'. This gain – or profit – may result in your paying capital gains tax.

There are lots of other taxes – like stamp duty when you buy a home – but none that you are likely to encounter for a few years.

Five useful things to know about the tax system

1. **Tax rates are set once a year.** The politician in charge of the tax system is the Chancellor of the Exchequer. Once a year he or she announces what the tax rates will be for the next year. This is done in a special speech to the House of Commons called the Budget Speech.

2. **Tax is collected by HM Revenue & Customs.** The government department responsible for collecting your tax and dealing with all tax matters is called Her Majesty's Revenue & Customs (HMRC).

3. **If you work for someone, your tax will be collected automatically.** If you have a job, then any tax you owe will be kept by your employer and sent to the Inland Revenue. This system is called Pay As You Earn, or PAYE.

4. **If you work for yourself, you must pay your own tax.** If you are self-employed, you must look after your own tax affairs. Once a year you will have to fill out a tax form and tell the Inland Revenue how much money you have made. Then you must send them

any tax you owe. This is called the self-assessment system.

5. **Tax has to be paid by individuals and by businesses.** Businesses have to pay tax, too. This is called corporation tax.

Your entitlement to state benefits

We are lucky enough to live in a country that looks after its citizens extremely well with all sorts of cash and other benefits for those in need. What's more, many of these benefits are available to you from the age of 16 onwards.

Here is a summary of all the main benefits to which you may be entitled. As benefits change all the time, you should contact the appropriate organisation, government department or service for the latest details.

Money to study

If you are over 16, have done your GCSEs and want to continue at school or college, then you may be eligible for a special payment of up to £30 a week.

The Educational Maintenance Allowance (EMA) is a new scheme designed to encourage young people of school age to continue with their education. To be eligible, you must be at least 16 (in some areas 17) at the start of the academic year and your family's total annual household income must be under £30,810. If you are eligible for an EMA, you will receive the payment straight into your bank account and you can spend it as you choose. Additional bonuses of up to £100 cash are also available.

You should also be aware of the Transport Support scheme, which is designed to help with transport to and from your school or college, and the Learner Support Fund, which is designed to assist with transport, books, equipment, childcare provision and even the cost of living away from home.

If you would like to know more about any of these benefits, you should contact your nearest Department for Children, Schools and Families office or visit their website at www.dfes.gov.uk.

Extra money if you are disabled

There are a whole range of different benefits you and/or your carers could receive if you are disabled, depending on the amount of care you need and whether you are working, studying or unemployed. For more information contact the Department for Work and Pensions – you'll find their telephone number in the phone book – or visit their website at www.dwp.gov.uk.

Extra income if you are struggling financially

If you are struggling financially, you may be able to claim Income Support benefit, which is available from the age of 16 onwards. For more information contact the Department for Work and Pensions – you'll find their telephone number in the phone book – or visit their website at www.dwp.gov.uk.

Housing benefit is also paid to people on a low income for help towards their rent, as is Council Tax benefit. Contact your local council for more information.

The Working Tax Credit also helps people in work who are on a low income. If you are responsible for a child or are disabled and work at least 16 hours a week, you may be able to claim, providing you are aged 16 or over. However, if you don't have responsibility for a child or you aren't disabled, you must be at least 25 years old and work for 30 hours to qualify. For more information contact your local HM Revenue & Customs office or visit their website at www.hmrc.gov.uk.

Free healthcare

In addition to the normal range of free healthcare available under the National Health Service (NHS) if you are under 16, or under 19 in full-time education, on Income Support or income-based Jobseeker's Allowance, you may be able to claim:

- → vouchers towards the cost of glasses or contact lenses
- → travel costs to and from hospital for NHS treatment
- → free prescriptions
- → free dental check-ups and treatment
- → free eye tests.

If you would like to know more about any of these benefits, you should contact your local social security office or call the Health Benefits Line on 0845 850 1166.

Money while you are looking for a job

If you have left school and are looking for work, then you may be eligible for the Jobseeker's Allowance. This is normally only given to those aged over 18 and is paid if you are 'capable of working, available for work and actively looking for work'. Once you have been claiming this allowance for six months or more if you are aged between 18 and 24, you will have to enrol in the 'New Deal' for young people. This programme is designed to offer you advice, guidance, work experience, training and other opportunities designed to ensure you find full-time employment. If you refuse to take part in this programme, you are likely to lose your Jobseeker's Allowance and any other benefits you may be claiming.

In certain circumstances the Jobseeker's Allowance may be payable to those aged 16 and over. For instance, if you have a good reason for not living with your parents, if you are temporarily laid off work, if you are a parent, if you are waiting for a suitable training place and so forth.

Incidentally, if you are under 18 and not being supported by your parents, your local social services are obliged to support you financially.

If you would like to know more about the Jobseeker's Allowance, you should contact your local Jobcentre Plus. If you think you may be eligible for support by your local social services, you should contact your local authority. The relevant government department is the Department for Work and Pensions, which will have a local office near you. Their website is www.dwp.gov.uk.

If you are pregnant or a parent

If you are working and pregnant, your employer is legally obliged to provide you with maternity pay for 26 weeks. If you haven't been employed or if you haven't paid National Insurance for a set number of weeks, you may be entitled to Maternity Allowance. If you are a new father, you may also be able claim two weeks' paid paternity leave. Finally, if you are bringing up a child under 16 (or under 19 and studying full time), you are entitled to claim child benefit of £16.50 for the first child and £11.05 for each other child. You may also be eligible for Child Tax Credit. To learn more, visit the government information website at www.direct.gov.uk.

More information

There are various other sources of information and help you may find useful, including:

Citizens Advice will provide you with free legal and financial help. Their website is packed with useful information, or look in the telephone book for your nearest branch. You can visit their website at www.adviceguide. org.uk.

The government has created a special website to help you find information about your rights (as well as the law) quickly and easily at www.direct.gov.uk.

Connexions is for you if you are 13–19, living in England and want advice on getting to where you want to be in life. It also provides support up to the age of 25 for young people who have learning difficulties or disabilities (or both). There are links to equivalent services in Scotland, Wales and Northern Ireland on the Connexions website at www.connexions-direct.com.

Jobcentre Plus should be your first port of call if you are looking for full- or part-time work. The team there will also be able to help explain some of the benefits you may be entitled to claim. The Jobcentre Plus website is at www. jobcentreplus.gov.uk.

1	It is important you know the law when you start working so that you don't get taken advantage of.
2	Once you reach school-leaving age, you are treated as an adult and enjoy the same rights.
3	The purpose of a payslip is to explain what pay you are receiving – and why.
4	You can't avoid paying some tax, but you can make sure you don't pay more than you have to.
5	If you are ill, unemployed, homeless, on a low income, struggling to find the money to study, pregnant, a parent or in need of medical care, the state will provide you with financial help.

3

LONG-TERM
money matters

13 Buying your own home

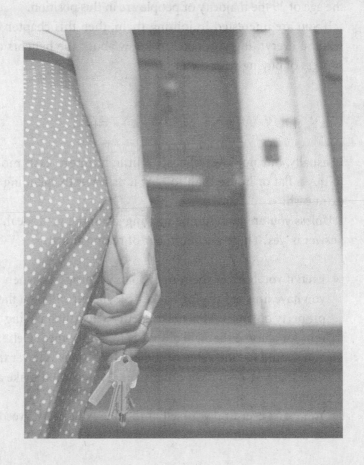

Have you ever dreamed of owning your own home?

It could be something that happens sooner than you expect. Because not only do more and more people choose to buy their own homes but also they are getting younger and younger when they do it.

Nowadays, it isn't so unusual to be in your early 20s when you first put your foot on what is often called the 'property ladder'. Indeed, one in five adults under 25 owns their own home and by the age of 29 the majority of people are in this position.

If you are interested in joining them, then this chapter will tell you everything you need to know about the benefits and process of buying your own home.

Why buy when you can rent?

It usually, but not always, costs a little bit more each month to buy a flat or house than to rent it. Is it worth spending the extra cash?

Unless you are going to be moving around a great deal, the answer is 'yes'. There are a number of reasons for this:

→ Even if you borrow the money to buy a property, when you have finished paying back the loan you will own the property outright. This makes better sense than paying rent for a home that will always belong to someone else.
→ You should see the value of the property increase over the time that you own it. In other words, you should make a profit.
→ You won't ever find yourself at the mercy of nasty, greedy or useless landlords.

Buying your own home is one of the best investments it is possible to make.

Finding the money to buy a property

Unless you are very wealthy, you will need to borrow money to buy your own home. Almost everyone does this by taking out a 'mortgage' or 'home loan' (these expressions both mean the same thing).

Mortgages – special loans to buy property – offer two clear benefits to buyers:

1. The monthly repayments are low when you consider the amount of money you are borrowing. This is because mortgages can be repaid over a very long period of time: 25 or even 30 years if you want.
2. The rate of interest charged is low. This is because mortgages are just about the cheapest type of borrowing there is.

The reason why mortgage interest rates are lower than other loan interest rates is because mortgages are 'secured loans'. A secured loan is one where the lender has 'security' – almost always property – that can be sold to repay the loan if the borrower stops his or her payments for any reason. Not that lenders like selling a property in order to get their money back. They will wait months, even years, before taking such drastic action. Still, it gives them peace of mind and this in turn means that borrowers benefit from much lower interest charges.

Incidentally, the length of a mortgage is called its 'term'. So if you borrow money for 25 years this is a 25-year term.

How much can you borrow?

How much you can borrow will be linked to how much you earn and how much of your own money you invest in the property. Whatever you put in towards buying the property is called your 'deposit'.

Mortgages can be arranged with banks, building societies and other financial institutions and each lender has its own rules. Broadly speaking, however, you can borrow the following amounts:

→ **3.5 to 5 times your gross income,** if you are buying the property alone
→ **2.5 or more times the gross income of all the people buying the property,** if you are buying it with someone else.

Here 'gross income' means the amount you earn every year before you pay tax.

Let's look at a couple of examples. If you are buying the property by yourself and your annual salary is £20,000, then you should easily be able to borrow £70,000 (£20,000 x 3.5). If you are buying the property with your partner and one of you earns £20,000 and the other earns £15,000, then you should easily be able to borrow £87,500 (£20,000 + £15,000 = £35,000 x 2.5).

Some lenders will let you borrow the full purchase price of the property. This is called a '100% mortgage'. If you were buying a flat costing £80,000 with a 100% mortgage, you could borrow £80,000, providing you earned enough income to make the repayments. However, 100% mortgages are much more expensive than other types of mortgage and aren't generally a good idea.

So how much deposit will you need? To get the best deal, probably at least 15% of the value of the property you want to buy. This would mean, if you were buying a £100,000 property, that you would have to have a deposit of £15,000 and enough income to pay an £85,000 mortgage.

Price of property	£100,000
15% deposit	less (£15,000)
Mortgage	£85,000

However, it is also possible to get 90% and 95% mortgages.

A much cheaper option ...

If you don't think you are going to be able to afford to buy a house by yourself, then try the housing associations in your area. Many offer schemes that allow you to buy a property at well below its true value. To find local housing associations look in the *Yellow Pages*, visit your nearest Citizens Advice Bureau or contact the Housing Corporation. Telephone: 0845 230 7000; website: **www. housingcorp.gov.uk**.

Other costs when you buy a home

Buying a home costs more than just the price of the property. You will also need extra cash to pay for:

→ a survey and valuation: a surveyor will look at the property for you to make sure it is in a good condition; they will also tell you whether it is worth what you are paying for it
→ legal fees: you will have to pay a solicitor to check that the property really belongs to the person selling it and to make sure the purchase proceeds smoothly
→ stamp duty: this is a government tax that many homebuyers have to pay
→ insurance: you will need to insure the house and its contents. Your mortgage lender may want you to take out extra insurance, too.

All of this will come to several thousand pounds. Any bank or building society will help you work out the exact cost.

Which mortgage should you choose?

There are lots of different types of mortgages available, but they can all be divided into two groups.

The first group is made up of 'repayment' (or 'annuity') mortgages. With this type of mortgage, your monthly repayments are divided into two parts. The first part is the interest you owe on the total amount borrowed. The second part is the repayment of part of the capital you have borrowed. The big advantage of this mortgage is that you are guaranteed to have paid off your whole loan at the end of the agreed period. However, in the early years almost all your monthly repayments will be in interest.

The other sort of mortgage on offer is an 'interest-only' mortgage. With this type of mortgage, you pay only the interest for the agreed period. At the same time, you would normally set up a savings plan, which is supposed to pay off the loan at the end of the agreed term. Your monthly repayments will, therefore, consist of interest on the loan and a contribution to a savings plan.

For most people a repayment mortgage is the safer, more sensible option.

More choices to make

As if you didn't have enough choice already, another decision to make when mortgage shopping can be whether to opt for a 'fixed' or 'variable' interest rate.

A fixed interest rate means that the amount of interest you pay is preset for an agreed period of time. So even if interest rates rise, your repayments will stay the same. Fixed-interest mortgages tend to be a little bit more expensive and if interest rates fall you won't benefit.

A variable interest rate, on the other hand, will move with the market. This is fine while interest rates are low but if they begin to rise it could be bad news.

Your home is not the most expensive thing you will buy

It is worth remembering your home won't necessarily be the most expensive thing you buy. Depending on interest rates, that honour could easily go to your mortgage. This is one of the reasons why it is crucial you choose the least expensive mortgage option available to you.

The rate of interest you are charged on your mortgage makes a HUGE difference to the total cost of your home.

For instance, if you pay 6.5% instead of 5.5% on a £100,000 mortgage lasting 25 years, it could cost you over £18,000 extra. Think how much extra you would have to earn after tax to end up with £18,000 in your pocket. Paying more mortgage interest than you have to – even 1% a year – can seriously damage your wealth. Shopping around makes excellent sense.

A tip worth remembering

If you ever take out a mortgage, look at the possibility of making extra payments each month and shortening the time it takes you to repay the whole amount. You may find that you can own your home outright much faster and save yourself a lot of interest, too.

Rent out a room

If you want to buy a property and you haven't got enough money to make the monthly repayments, consider renting out one of the rooms for extra cash. This is how lots of people get started.

The different stages of buying a home

There are nine steps to buying a home and they are best explained with an example.

1. Work out how much you have to spend

Richard earns £18,000 a year. Judy earns £15,000 a year. Between them and with help from their families they have managed to save £14,000. They are putting £4,000 of this to one side to pay for solicitors and other costs leaving them with a deposit of

£10,000. They have worked out they can comfortably borrow £82,500, so the maximum they have to spend is £92,500.

2. Find a solicitor
Before they even start looking, Richard and Judy have spoken to a solicitor and agreed with him how much he is going to charge.

3. Find a property you like
Richard and Judy live in Liverpool. Although there are houses within their price range, they are a long way from where both of them work. Instead they have opted for a flat costing £85,000.

4. Make an offer
The solicitor looking after Richard and Judy got in touch with the estate agent selling the property and made an offer of £78,000 on the flat. After several days of going backwards and forwards, the person selling the flat (called the 'vendor') agreed to take £81,000.

5. Shop around for the best mortgage deal
While the solicitor was agreeing the price, Richard and Judy searched for the best mortgage deal. In the end they chose a building society. Richard and Judy completed a written application form.

6. Wait for the surveyor's report
The building society arranged for the flat to be surveyed and valued by a professional property expert – and so did Richard and Judy. Both experts said it was in good condition and worth what Richard and Judy were paying for it.

7. Wait for the solicitors to do their stuff

The seller's solicitor sent a contract to Richard and Judy's solicitor, who checked that everything was legal and that the building society had agreed to make the loan. Richard and Judy gave their solicitor the £14,000 deposit.

8. Exchange contracts

When the solicitors had agreed everything was ready, the first part of the buying process took place. This is called 'exchange of contracts'. Richard and Judy's solicitor paid 10% of the purchase price to the seller's solicitor to guarantee the deal.

9. Completion!

Four weeks later, Richard and Judy's building society paid the loan money to their solicitor, who passed it on to the seller's solicitor. On the same day the rest of the paperwork was completed. The seller moved out and Richard and Judy moved in. This whole process is called 'completion'.

1	Buying your home is one of the best investments it is possible to make and a surprisingly high percentage of first-time buyers are in their early 20s.
2	If you can't afford to buy a house yourself, try contacting your local housing association, which may be able to help.

14 Your worst money enemy and how to defeat it

What could possibly stop you from having enough money to live the sort of life you dream of?

The answer may surprise you.

It is borrowing money.

I am not talking about reckless borrowing, either, but ordinary borrowing in the form of personal loans, overdrafts and credit cards.

This is because the cost of borrowing money is a huge drain on your most valuable asset – your income.

What's more, the cost of borrowing can't just be measured in terms of the interest you will have to pay. When you spend all your available cash on repaying loans, you miss out on the chance to invest it and make yourself better off.

Let me give you one simple example:

→ If you borrow £5,000 over a period of seven years at an interest rate of 15%, it will mean monthly loan repayments of about £96.
→ If you invested £96 a month into, say, the stock market for the same period of seven years (assuming growth at 9%), it would be worth in the region of £11,000.

In other words, borrowing has two costs. The cost of the interest and the cost of the lost opportunity to do something else with your money.

From the age of 18 you are in a position to borrow a great deal of money. In this chapter we will look at what this means to you, and what to do if you ever find your borrowing has got a little out of hand.

Why it isn't good to be in debt

Most people borrow money but fail to think of themselves as being in debt. The fact is:

→ you don't have to be having money problems to be in debt: a loan is not a loan; it is a debt
→ debt is the single greatest threat to your financial freedom and security: it is sucking away your most valuable asset – your income
→ the first benefit of being debt-free is that your money becomes your own to spend or invest as you prefer
→ when you are in debt, you have less choice: you must work to pay it back
→ when you are in debt, you are vulnerable: you can't afford to have other money problems, like being unable to work because you are ill.

Debt is becoming a huge problem

In recent years people have been borrowing more and more money. For instance:

→ Students are leaving university with an average of £10,000 debt.
→ The average household owes nearly £8,000 of debt and this is before you add in mortgages.

Why are people borrowing so much?

Some borrowing can't be helped, for example if you need to buy a car to get to work.

Some can be put down to factors such as changing social values, lack of education at school, our consumer society and 'impulse' spending.

Some must be because interest rates, in general, are quite low at the moment, making it cheaper to borrow.

The biggest reason for the borrowing boom, however, may well be that debt has become a hugely profitable business. Banks and other financial institutions are using clever marketing tricks to push debt onto innocent consumers. They are doing this because the returns are irresistible. Look how much money they can make:

If you leave money on deposit at a bank, you'll typically earn in the region of 2% (£2 for every £100) a year by way of interest.
That bank, however, can lend your money to someone else at anything up to 16% or more (£16 or more for every £100) interest a year.

Is it any wonder that banks are falling over themselves to lend money? Or that they devote so much energy to coming up with new ways to sell loans to their customers?

Debt comes in many disguises

Many people believe that, providing they are never behind on their repayments, they are not in debt. This isn't true. A debt is when you owe someone money. It could be:

→ an unpaid balance on a credit card
→ an overdraft
→ a personal loan
→ a car loan or loan for some other specific purchase
→ a mortgage on your home
→ a secured loan
→ a hire-purchase agreement
→ an unpaid balance on a store charge card
→ a business loan
→ a loan made by a friend or family member.

The first step to getting out of debt

If you ever find yourself worried about the amount of debt you have, the first thing to do is simple: stop borrowing. After all, you can't get yourself out of a hole if you keep digging. Take a once-and-for-all decision to:

→ not just pay off your debts but stay out of debt
→ not borrow any more money unless it is absolutely unavoidable
→ not live beyond your means.

There are various actions you can take to make this easier on yourself, including:

→ cutting up all your credit cards and store cards
→ letting your lenders know you have a problem and need help
→ cancelling your overdraft limit
→ not buying anything you don't need
→ not increasing the size of any existing loans.

If you are having problems, then try keeping a money diary. Carry a small notebook with you wherever you go and write down details of every single penny you spend. After a couple of weeks, you'll have a precise picture of where your money is going and this, in turn, may help you avoid spending money on things you don't really want or need.

Sizing up the problem

Once you have stopped making the situation any worse, you need to gather together full details of all your debts. The information you require about each of your debts includes:

→ to whom you owe the money
→ how big the debt is
→ how long you have to pay it back (the term), if relevant
→ what the rate of interest is and whether it is fixed or variable
→ whether it will cost you anything extra to pay the debt back early
→ what the minimum monthly payment is (if this is relevant).

Most of the information you need should be supplied to you each month by your lenders. However, if it isn't, then you should telephone or write to them asking for full details.

Paying all your debts off – quickly and easily

You've taken the decision not to incur any extra debt. You've got a real grip on the size and nature of your problem. What next? You have two options:

Option one: the consolidation approach

The idea behind 'consolidation' is to dramatically reduce the cost of your debt and then to pay it off faster.

How?

By consolidating, or lumping together, all your loans at a much lower interest rate.

So, instead of having lots of different loans – all at different rates – you have a single loan at one, much lower rate.

What you do is:

→ add up all the money you currently spend making your debt repayments
→ take out a new loan at a lower rate of interest and use this money to pay off all your other debts
→ keep on making the same monthly payments that you were making before.

By keeping up the same monthly payments, you can really speed yourself out of debt.

This approach works best if you own your own home, because you can take out a secured loan or consolidate your loans in with your mortgage.

Option two: the sniper approach

If you don't own your own home – or if you don't have sufficient capital tied up in your property to consolidate your debts in with your mortgage – you'll probably need to take the 'sniper' approach. This involves 'picking off' your debts one at a time, starting with the most expensive. What you do is:

→ move as much of your borrowing as you can to where it is costing you the least: this is a sort of 'mini' consolidation

→ use the money you are saving each month to pay off your most expensive debt – in other words, the one with the highest rate of interest.

Do you sometimes pay more than the minimum amount required each month? If you do, then make sure you pay it to whichever of your debts is costing you the most. Incidentally, you may find that one or more of your existing lenders will be open to the idea of lowering the rate of interest they are charging you. If they think you might take your loan elsewhere, they might be happy to talk about a better deal.

If you have serious debt problems

If you are unfortunate enough to have serious debt problems, there are a number of non-profit (charitable) organisations that will help you for free:

Citizens Advice Bureau
Look in your local telephone book.
Website: **www.nacab.org.uk**

Consumer Credit Counselling Service
Telephone: 0800 138 1111
Website: **www.cccs.co.uk**

National Debtline
Freephone: 0808 808 4000
Website: **www.nationaldebtline.co.uk**

Be careful of so-called 'debt counsellors' who offer to help you for a fee. Most of these will rip you off.

1	Borrowing has two costs. The cost of the interest and the cost of the lost opportunity to do something else with your money.
2	If lenders believe you might take your loan business elsewhere, they'll often agree to a better deal.

15 Money-making secrets

If you want to build up a bit of money, the thing to do is save on a regular basis.

But if you want to make your money really grow, then you need to make it work much harder.

Finding ways to make your money work much harder for you is called 'investing', and in this chapter we will be looking at:

→ how to become a successful investor
→ some different investment options
→ tax-free investments
→ how to start your own investment club.

As you will discover, making money from your money can be rewarding in more ways than one, because investment doesn't have to be a boring business. You could, for instance, buy stocks and shares, gold, stamps, wine or classic motorbikes. What's more, teenagers who develop an interest in investment often turn out to be better at it than the professionals.

You don't need a lot of money to start

There is no rule that says you should have a certain amount of money before you start investing. In fact, you could:

→ invest a lump sum
→ invest a regular amount each week or month
→ invest whatever spare cash you can whenever it suits you.

Whether you have £1 to invest or £100,000, it makes no difference.

However, you shouldn't invest money that you might need in an emergency, because the best investments require you to lock your money away for a long period. Usually, but not always, the longer you leave your money locked away, the more profit you will make.

You control the risk

One of the first questions every investor has to ask him- or herself is: how much risk am I willing to take?

In general, the more cautious you are, the less reward (or profit) you can expect. Whereas, if you are willing to take a greater risk, you will be in with the chance of a much higher reward.

A bank deposit account is not at all risky. But your reward will only be a small amount of interest every year.

Gambling on a horse, on the other hand, is very risky. If it loses the race, you lose all your money. But if it wins, you could make a huge profit.

Of course, a bank deposit account is one of the safest investments you could make, whereas gambling on a horse is one of the riskiest. Happily, there are lots of different options in between.

How do you balance risk and reward? Should you accept a lower profit in exchange for peace of mind? Or should you try and make your money grow more quickly and face the possibility of losses? The answer may be: neither. The secret of successful investment is to:

→ set yourself some goals, look at all the options and then decide which investments will give you what you are looking for
→ not put all your money in one place but divide it up between different sorts of investment: this is called 'diversifying'
→ not change your mind all the time
→ stay on top of it: keep an eye on how your investments are doing for you.

Decide on how much money you are going to invest

If you are saving regularly, then you will have a choice between:

→ investing in a specially designed long-term savings plan
→ building up blocks of capital ('capital' is another word for lump sums of money) and investing each one somewhere different.

If you have a lump sum – or as you build up blocks of capital – then the choice of investments available to you opens up.

Have a clear idea in your mind about how much you plan to invest.

Decide how long you can tie your money up for

Is there a date you need your money back? In other words, are you investing for something specific or just to build your overall wealth?

Investments have varying degrees of 'liquidity'. Liquidity means how quickly you can sell your investment and get your money back.

An investment that allows you to get at your money immediately is called 'liquid'. Cash in a deposit account, for instance, is liquid.

An investment that may take a long time to sell is called 'illiquid'. Property, for instance, is illiquid.

How long you stay with any particular investment will depend on two things:

→ The type of investment. A five-year savings plan is – unless you break the rules – a five-year savings plan.
→ What happens! At some point there may be a good reason to sell your investment.

Bear in mind that regular savings products have advantages and disadvantages. On the one hand, they tie you in so that if you need your money in an emergency you may lose some or all of your profit. On the other hand, they force you to be disciplined about saving.

Decide how much profit you are looking for

Will you be happy with a small but steady return? Or are you after bigger gains? You need to have an idea of what you are looking for when you choose your investments.

Some investments come with 'guaranteed returns'. This means that you can be 100% certain what profit you are going to make, and when. In general, however, you will have to decide the value of an investment for yourself. Something that may help you do this is 'past performance' – what sort of profits an investment made in the past. You can't count on the same thing happening again, but the information will still be useful.

Two mistakes to avoid

Investors often make two mistakes that could easily be avoided. First of all, they invest more money than they can afford. Then, when they are stuck for cash, they sell their investment in a hurry. Secondly, they chop and change their mind, putting their cash into one thing and then another. In both cases, the result is the same: they don't make much of a profit (or may even make a loss).

How to find suitable investment opportunities

You have decided that you want to start investing. Where can you look for suitable opportunities? Who can you trust for advice? Chapter 18 provides detailed suggestions on getting financial advice. Meanwhile, you may like to consider some of the following options:

→ your bank or building society
→ national newspapers and their websites
→ special money and investment magazines and websites.

All sorts of organisations from banks to supermarkets offer investment opportunities. A good place to look for general advice is in your local library, which should carry a range of investment books and magazines.

A few investment options

What follows is a brief description of some of the most popular types of investment and also some 'alternative' investments, such as collectibles and stamps.

It is never too early to start buying stocks and shares
How would you like to own part of your favourite company or companies?

That's what you will be doing if you start buying 'shares'. Because a share (also called 'stock') is, literally, a share in a company's wealth.

So if you own a share in, say, Ford, you own a tiny part of their factories, showrooms, unsold cars, bank accounts and everything else that they own. Plus, you are entitled to a share of any profits that Ford makes each year.

Of course, the value of a share in any particular company may go up or down depending on all sorts of things, like how good the managers are, the sort of products they sell, their volume of sales and so forth.

This makes buying some shares risky.

The least risky shares, by the way, are called 'blue chip'. Blue-chip companies are the ones that tend to do best and their shares tend to be the most expensive.

Shares are bought and sold in the stock market. Most countries have stock markets and some, like the United States, have several.

If you only have a limited amount of money, then buying shares may not make sense, because:

→ you will have to pay commission (a fee) every time you buy and sell and the commission can easily wipe out your profits
→ shares, even blue-chip shares, can be quite risky.

On the other hand, buying and selling shares is fun! What's more, over the longer term, the stock market has produced bigger profits for investors than just about any other form of investment. And, if you buy shares in profitable companies, not only should you see the share price go up but you should also enjoy an income. This income, which is your share of the profits, is called a 'dividend'. Companies usually pay out a dividend once or twice a year.

How do you pick shares to buy?

The best way to find shares to buy is to do your own homework. First of all, look in the business sections of the national newspapers for information. Secondly, contact companies you are interested in and ask them to send you information and – especially – their annual report. They will do this for free. Thirdly, keep your eyes peeled for businesses you think are doing well and then find out more about them. You will also find a lot of information on the Internet, and your bank or building society should be able to help, too.

Getting started

To buy and sell shares, you will need to open an account with a stockbroker – a firm that specialises in buying and selling shares and also in offering stock-market advice. The cheapest way will almost definitely be to buy and sell online, and if you search for UK stockbrokers you'll get plenty of choices. All the major banks offer stockbroking, as do many of the building societies. If you want a complete list, contact the London Stock Exchange (LSE), 10 Paternoster Square, London EC4M 7LS, telephone 020 7797 1000 or visit their website at **www.londonstockexchange.com**.

HOW TO READ THE FINANCIAL PAGES

If you do decide to buy stocks and shares, you can keep track of their performance by reading the stock-market pages in your daily newspaper. Next to the name of your company you'll find the following information:

high	low	stock	price	change	yield	P/E
1184.00	979.50	3i	1038.00	-2.00	1.8	4.1
226.75	150.00	Aberdeen Asset	175.75	-0.25	2.8	27.4
1195.00	668.50	Admiral Group	878.50	-1.00	3.4	22.1
155.00	122.50	Aefis Group	130.25	+0.25	1.5	19.2

High. This is the highest price (in pence) that your particular company share has reached in the past 12 months.

Low. This is the lowest price that your share has reached in the past 12 months.

Price. This is the average price paid for your share at close of business on the previous day.

Change. This is usually represented by a (+) or (-) symbol, and it lets you know how much your share increased or fell by in the previous day's trading.

Yield. This percentage figure tells you how valuable the dividend from your share is. The higher the dividend yield, the better. (When you own shares in a company, you are entitled to a dividend, or share of the profits – if there are profits to be shared, that is.)

P/E. This stands for 'price earnings ratio', and it is one of the methods experts use to value a share.

Pooled investments

Investing in the stock market is a good way to make money – but it has some drawbacks:

→ There is so much choice it can be difficult to decide which shares to buy and also when to sell them.

→ You need a lot of money to buy a good selection of

shares – which in turn is the best way to avoid risk.
→ You have to pay commission every time you buy and sell shares. If you are only buying in small quantities, then this commission can easily wipe out your profits.

The solution? Let a professional invest your money for you via a 'pooled investment'.

Pooled investments come in many forms, with names like 'unit trusts' and 'managed funds', but they all work on the same basis:

Your money – along with the money of all the other people taking part – is pooled and then invested. Each pooled investment fund has different objectives. For instance, one might invest in the largest UK companies, another in European companies, a third in Korean property and so forth. In each case the fund managers – the people running the fund and making the investment decisions – will indicate the type of risk involved. They will also provide you, on a regular basis, with written reports or statements explaining how your money is performing.

Pooled investments are ideal for smaller investors, but watch out for the charges that some fund managers make. Remember, too, not all fund managers are good at what they do – so pick your fund carefully.

Pooled investments should be thought of as medium- to long-term investment vehicles. In other words, you should plan to leave your money in them for an absolute minimum of five years – and more like ten years or even longer.

Consider the tax-free benefits of an ISA

In order to encourage saving and investment, the government has created something called an Individual Savings Account – or ISA, for short – which offers you the chance to make money without paying tax.

ISAs allow you to invest in all sorts of ways – from bank deposit accounts to stock and shares – but the rules are quite complicated.

Why not start an investment club?

If you'd like to dabble in the stock market but only have a relatively small amount of money to invest, why not start an investment club? An investment club is when a group of friends or work colleagues pool their resources and make buying and selling decisions together. Investment clubs regularly outperform the stock market, because those involved take a real and detailed interest in every investment decision.

If you would like to know more about this, Proshare Investment Clubs, 3rd Floor, 8–11 Lime Street, London, EC3M 7AA will help you. Visit their website at **www.proshareclubs.co.uk**.

If you would like more information, ask at any bank or building society or visit the Financial Services Authority website at www.fsa.gov.uk.

Some alternative investments

Most investors, wisely, stick to traditional homes for their money. Stocks and shares, savings plans and property, for instance. A growing number, however, like to invest in something different. These are called 'alternative investments' and tend to come in and out of fashion. One year it will be vintage wines and pop memorabilia; the next, classic cars and racehorses.

The idea of putting your money into such investments is by no means new. In the 17th century in Holland many people put their money into tulip bulbs. Prices soared and then – very suddenly – collapsed. This highlights a great lesson for anyone interested in alternative investment: once prices have started to rise quickly, it is probably dangerous to start buying. If you are going to make money and avoid risk, you want to buy before anyone else has spotted the opportunity.

Other tips for anyone interested in alternative investments include:

➜ Make sure that what you are buying is in limited supply. The less of something there is, the better it is likely to hold its value.

→ Watch out for extra expenses. It might be fun (and not that expensive) to club together with friends and buy a greyhound for racing, but will the kennelling costs be high?

→ Make sure there will be some way to sell your investment when the time comes.

It is also worth remembering that if you have a personal interest in whatever you are buying you won't ever be disappointed because you can always enjoy owning the item.

Alternative investments should only be made once you have money invested more safely elsewhere. Why? Because they are all – without exception – high risk. Here are a few examples of investments that can definitely be considered alternative:

→ Antiques
→ Art
→ Coins
→ Classic cars and motorbikes
→ Collectibles
→ Costumes from famous films
→ Fishing memorabilia
→ Gold
→ Greyhounds
→ Modern furniture
→ Platinum
→ Pop memorabilia

➜ Precious stones such as diamonds
➜ Racehorses
➜ Stamps
➜ Wine

1	Teenagers who develop an interest in investment often turn out to be better at it than professionals.
2	If you own a share in, say, Ford, you own a tiny part of their factories, showrooms, unsold cars, bank accounts and everything else that they own.
3	An Individual Savings Account offers you a chance to make money without paying a penny in tax.

16 Get protected

Life is a risky business. Every day, all around us, terrible things are happening. Some of these terrible things happen to possessions. For instance:

→ houses burn down
→ cars crash
→ roofs are blown off
→ holidays are cancelled because of strikes
→ bicycles are stolen.

Some of these terrible things happen to people. For instance, people:

→ fall ill
→ get hurt in accidents
→ die.

Obviously, some of the terrible things that can happen are worse than others.

Having your bicycle stolen is hardly as serious as breaking a leg and nowhere near as bad as dying. Every terrible thing that happens, however, will have financial consequences. For instance:

→ If you own something that is lost, damaged or stolen, you will have to spend money to replace it.
→ If you are ill or have an accident, you may be off work and unable to pay for all your living expenses.
→ If you die (especially when you are older and have a family), you may leave people behind who were depending on you to support them.

The idea of insurance is to make sure that, when something terrible happens, money is there to protect you from the financial cost. It works like this:

→ Every year you pay money to an insurance company. This money is called the 'annual premium' or just the 'premium'.

→ The amount you pay will depend on what you want insurance for. The cost of insuring a house from being burned down, for example, is much higher than the cost of insuring a bicycle from being stolen. There are many sorts of insurance available.

→ If whatever you have insured yourself against happens, then the insurance company will pay you an agreed amount of money, for instance enough money to rebuild your house or buy yourself another bicycle.

Broadly speaking, insurance divides into two types:

1. 'General' insurance. This pays out when something happens to possessions, such as cars, homes, pets, motorbikes, valuables and so forth. It also includes things like holiday insurance and accident insurance.

2. 'Life' insurance. This pays out when people fall very ill or die.

Examples of general insurance

Extended product warranties

When you buy something, the law protects you if it breaks down or is faulty – often even if it is second-hand. But your protection – which is called a 'warranty' – only lasts for a set period of time: usually a year for new items. If you want, you can pay to make the warranty last for a longer period of time, say three years. This type of insurance tends not to be good value for money. Don't let a salesman talk you into it unless you are really certain you want it.

Home contents cover

As its name suggests, this insurance pays out if anything in your home – the contents, in fact – is lost, damaged or stolen. This is important insurance to have. Also, it often protects your possessions when they are out of your home. For instance, most policies cover bicycles. Whether you rent or buy your home, it is worthwhile to arrange home contents insurance.

Buildings cover

This type of insurance protects the 'fabric' of your home – the walls, ceilings, roof, windows, floors and so forth – against damage or total loss as a result of a fire, flood or some other disaster. If you rent your home, you don't have to worry about buildings cover – it is for the owner to arrange.

Private medical insurance

Although most medical treatment is available free from the National Health Service (NHS), it is possible to arrange private care. This means you choose when and where you are treated and by whom. To help pay for this it is possible to take out private medical insurance.

Motor cover

This protects your car in the event of an accident or theft.

See the special section for more information.

Motor breakdown cover

If your car breaks down, this insurance pays for a mechanic to come and look at it and, if necessary, for a tow-truck to take the car (and you) home. It is offered by organisations such as the RAC and the AA.

Other types of cover

Other sorts of protection include motorbike cover (if your motorbike is damaged or stolen), caravan cover (if your caravan is damaged or stolen), boat cover (if your boat is lost or stolen), pet protection cover (to pay for your pet's vet bills), travel cover (protecting you when you go overseas) and dozens of other specialist insurance plans.

Buying car insurance

The good news is that once you turn 17 you can apply for a provisional driving licence, allowing you to learn to drive.

The bad news is that when you are behind the wheel of anything other than a driving-school car you are going to need special car insurance. And car insurance for anyone in their late teens or early 20s – with or without a full licence – is very, very expensive. In fact, it is not unheard of for the insurance to cost more than a decent second-hand car.

Happily, however, there are things you can do to bring your insurance costs down.

Car insurance made simple

Car insurance is there to protect you from the financial consequences of having a car accident. It means that if you are unfortunate enough to be responsible for a car crash you won't have to put your hand in your pocket. And, if someone else is responsible, you won't have to chase him or her to pay for the damage they have caused.

There are two different types of car insurance.

1. Third-party, fire and theft

Third-party, fire and theft insurance provides you with three different type of protection.

First of all, and most importantly, the 'third party' bit covers any claims made against you if you (a) injure or kill someone, (b) damage or destroy someone else's car and/or (c) damage or destroy someone else's property while you are driving. Don't ever be tempted to drive without third-party cover. Not only is it against the law (there's a fine of up to £5,000 and you could lose your licence) but also if you have an accident you will have to pay for any damage or compensation yourself.

Secondly, the 'fire' bit pays out if your car is damaged or destroyed by fire.

Finally, the 'theft' bit pays out if your car is stolen or damaged following an attempted theft.

Third-party, fire and theft insurance is the least expensive car insurance you can buy.

2. Comprehensive

Comprehensive insurance includes third-party, fire and theft cover plus it will also cover damage to your own car as a result of an accident.

Some comprehensive insurance includes extra benefits, such as:

→ replacement windscreen or windows if yours get damaged
→ the cost of any medical expenses if you or anyone travelling with you is injured while in the car
→ a replacement car if your car is in the garage being repaired
→ a lump sum of money if you die or are injured while using your car.

Comprehensive insurance can be quite a bit more expensive than third-party, fire and theft cover.

Check you are covered before you get behind the wheel

If you are learning to drive in someone else's car or – just as importantly – if you have passed your test and plan to drive someone else's car, MAKE SURE YOU ARE INSURED.

With most car insurance you have to be what is called a 'named' driver before you are allowed to drive someone else's car. This means the insurance company has added your name to the insurance policy.

Insurance doesn't provide total cover

It would be very rare for anyone making a claim on their insurance to receive every penny they ask for.

This is because most policies have something called an 'excess'. This is an amount of money that the insurance company expect you to pay if there is a claim. Suppose your excess is £100. If you put in a successful claim for £500 of damage, you will get £400 – that's £500 less the £100 excess. The bigger the excess, the less expensive the insurance.

You should also be aware that an insurance company's idea of what a car is worth and your own may differ. If you make a claim, expect at best to receive the car's 'market value', which is the same as its second-hand value. If you want to insure your car for what you paid for it (a good idea if you've borrowed money to buy it), you can take out something called Guaranteed Asset Protection (GAP) insurance.

How to keep the cost of car insurance down

The car insurance market is extremely competitive and so shopping around can make a huge difference to your annual 'premium' – which is what the bill for insurance cover is called. You must, however, be patient. Whether you search for a cheaper quotation by telephone or online, you will have to answer the same questions over and over again. In theory, an insurance broker should be able to find you the lowest price, but in reality many of the 'direct' insurance companies (so called because they only deal direct with the public) may be cheaper. If you want names of car insurance companies, try the national press and also your local *Yellow Pages*.

As a young driver it will be cheapest for you to be included on another, more experienced driver's policy. While being included on, for instance, your parents' car insurance may save you money, you should bear the following in mind:

→ If you have an accident and make a claim, the cost of insurance is likely to go up for whoever's car you were driving.

→ Insurance companies reward drivers who don't make claims by cutting the cost of their next year's premiums. So if you have the insurance in your own name and don't make a claim for two or three years, the cost of your cover will fall. Whereas, if you are included on someone else's policy, you won't see the benefit of your safe driving.

Finally, some insurers will offer you extra savings if you take the advanced driving test offered by the Institute of Advanced Motorists or if you participate in the Pass Plus scheme designed by the Driving Standards Agency.

Shopping for cheaper car insurance

When shopping around for cheaper insurance, it is worth remembering that insurance companies decide on the cost on the basis of how likely they think it is that you will make a claim. Some of the things that push the price of car insurance up include:

→ your age: younger people have more accidents
→ keeping the car in a city where there is more chance of an accident and more chance of it being stolen
→ leaving the car on the street overnight: cars locked up in garages are less likely to be stolen
→ fast and/or expensive cars: the bigger and more luxurious the car, the more your insurance will cost you; sports cars are also more costly to insure, especially if you are young
→ insuring the car with comprehensive cover: third-party, fire and theft is cheaper
→ making claims on your insurance policy.

The financial benefits of driving safely

Car insurance companies reward careful drivers with extra discounts on the annual cost of cover.

This discount is called a 'no-claims bonus' because you have to make no claims to the insurance company to receive it.

Every year that you don't make a claim, your bonus gets bigger. After one year without a claim you will have a one year's no-claims bonus, after two years you will have a two years' no-claims bonus and so forth, until after five years when you will have what is called the 'maximum no-claims bonus'.

A no-claims bonus can be a very valuable thing to have because it can bring down the cost of cover by up to three-quarters. So a £500 annual premium could cost you just £125.

After you have built up a few years' no-claims bonus, some car insurance companies will let you protect it by paying a little bit extra. If you have protected your no claims bonus in this way, you keep your no-claims discount even if you have an accident and make a claim.

Getting your car insured is a seven-step process

These are the different steps you will have to go through to get cover:

1. Draw up a list of all the insurance companies you want to get a quote from. Decide if you want third-party, fire and theft or comprehensive cover.
2. Telephone the insurance companies or visit their websites and supply details of your car and other information.
3. Choose the cheapest quotation – making sure you are comparing 'like for like'.
4. Complete an application form. This will either be

posted to you or will be on the insurance company's website.

5. Once your application has been submitted and accepted, you are usually covered immediately. You will be sent something called a 'cover note' to prove you have insurance.

6. Within a few days you will receive a pack containing your certificate of insurance and other information.

7. You usually have a choice of paying in one lump sum or over a few months. If you pay over a few months, it will probably cost you more.

Tell the truth!

When buying insurance, it is important to tell the truth. If you don't, and the insurance company find out, they may refuse to meet a claim and could withdraw your cover. Without insurance you will be responsible for paying out any claims against you. Also, you risk being taken to court by the police.

Protecting your most valuable assets

Mark Twain, a long-dead American writer, famously said: 'lies, damned lies and statistics' – and it is difficult to argue with him.

Statistics – a way of looking at things in terms of numbers – can be twisted to mean almost anything.

Still, there is no getting around certain facts. Every year an enormous number of people in Britain find themselves facing personal crises of one sort or another. Let me give you a few examples:

→ Almost one in five working-age households (that's a total of 3.4 million homes) include someone who is currently unemployed. In 2005 alone, 562,000 people were made redundant.
→ One in three people will be diagnosed with cancer at some point in their life.
→ Every two minutes someone in the country has a heart attack.
→ Every adult in Britain is five times more likely to suffer a serious disability than die before the age of 60.
→ 1,800,000 people in Britain are already disabled and have been unable to work for 12 months or more.

When anything dreadful happens – for instance not having a job, serious illness, an accident or (tragically) death – the last thing anyone wants is to have to think about money. Which is why, once you start working or taking on responsibilities, you should consider protecting yourself and your family from money worries.

How insurance can protect you and your family

There are two important situations where insurance could protect you (and your family should you have one) from money worries:

1. If you lose your income. Suppose you couldn't work because you were ill, had an accident or lost your job. How would you meet all your living expenses?
2. Death. Suppose you died, leaving behind a family or others who depend on you. How would they cope for money without you?

If you lose your income

If you can't earn money for reasons that are beyond your control (illness, an accident or redundancy – when you lose your job through no fault of your own), you will have to rely on your savings, your family, your employer (if you have one) and/or the state to support you. This may be fine, and then again it may not. This is why many people decide to take out some sort of income-protection insurance. Here is a brief summary of the two main sorts of policy on offer:

1. Critical illness cover.

You are more likely to suffer from a serious disease or life-threatening illness before you reach retirement than you are to die. Critical illness cover will protect you from this by paying you a lump sum if you contract cancer, heart attack, kidney failure, major organ transplant, multiple sclerosis, a stroke or various other conditions.

2. Income-protection insurance.

There are a number of options:

→ Mortgage payment protection. This will pay your mortgage for you if you are unable to work due to a major illness, accident, unemployment or failure of your business.
→ Credit or payment protection insurance. This is like mortgage insurance but for credit-card, personal-loan and other debts.
→ Accident, sickness and unemployment cover. This pays out under similar circumstances to mortgage payment protection – but there are no conditions attached to the money you receive.
→ Permanent health insurance. This pays out if you can't work because of illness or an accident and you receive the money until you recover, resume work or retire.

If you (or your partner) should die

There are, basically, two types of life cover designed to pay out money if the policyholder – the person insured   should die:

→ Term cover. This pays out a lump sum if you die before the term (usually 10, 15 or 20 years) of the policy is up. If you live, you don't get a penny back.
→ Whole-of-life cover. This protects you for the whole of your life – not just a limited term – and as a result it is much more expensive since the insurers know they are going to have to pay out one day!

Once you turn 18 you should think about writing a will

A will is a legal document that explains what you want done with your things after you die. It is the only way to make sure that the assets (your possessions) that you leave behind – including any life cover – end up with whoever you want to have them. When someone dies without writing a will, the result is months – if not years – of financial confusion and uncertainty. You can buy a will-writing pack from most major stationers or you can talk to a solicitor.

1	Insurance means that when something terrible happens money is there to cover the financial cost.
2	Insurance companies reward drivers who don't make a claim by cutting the cost of their next year's premiums.
3	When you start to take on family responsibilities, remember the value of protecting them – and yourself – with some inexpensive life cover.

17 How to retire early and RICH

You would have to be mad to think about something that isn't likely to happen for at least 40 years.

Or would you?

The 'something' I am talking about is how you will manage for money when you retire – by which I mean give up work.

And I can offer you three very powerful reasons why you should spend a few minutes thinking about it sooner rather than later:

1. You could live for a long, long time after you stop working. It isn't unusual for people to be retired for 30 years or more.
2. You can't rely on anyone else. The state pension system and many of the private pension schemes are in a mess and the situation is getting worse. Even what pensioners get today – which isn't much – may seem like a lot of money by the time you retire.
3. You will save a fortune if you start planning in your early 20s. Or, to put it the other way around, if you don't plan for your retirement in good time, you may have to carry on working until the day you die.

If this all strikes you as a bit negative and off-putting, here is another way to look at it:

With a little thought, you could easily be rich enough to stop working and spend your life doing exactly what you want while you are still young.

Right now, all you need to do is understand why it is important to plan for retirement, some of the options available to you and when you should take action.

A quick guide to the key terms

Retired. When you stop working full time, you are 'retired' or 'in retirement'.

Retirement age. This is the age when you can claim a state pension – currently 65 for men and between 60 and 65 for women, though by the time you retire it will be much higher.

Early retirement. Early retirement is if you retire before the retirement age.

Pension. This is money paid to you once you have retired.

State pension. This is money paid to you by the state after you reach the retirement age.

Private pension. If you make your own pension arrangement (basically, if you save money for when you are older in a pension savings scheme), this is called a private pension.

Company pension. If your employer agrees to pay you a pension when you retire, this is called a company pension.

What will happen if you do nothing?

If you (or your employer) don't make financial plans for your retirement, you will have to rely on the state. It is anyone's guess what that will mean by the time you reach the retirement age. If you were a single person retiring tomorrow, your basic state pension would be £84.25 a week.

£84.25 a week is not much money to pay for food, rent, electricity, telephone, gas, heating, clothes and entertainment. True, today's pensioners are entitled to other benefits and do get various perks – such as free or discounted travel on public transport – but, unless they have savings or some other sort of pension, they can expect to live in poverty.

A crisis in the making

You may have noticed references in the newspapers and on television to the 'pensions crisis'. This crisis is made up of a number of different elements.

First of all, the government has promised millions and millions of public sector workers (basically people who work for the state, like teachers and civil servants) that when they retire they will receive a pension linked to their earnings. This would be fine, except that the state hasn't put aside the money to pay for this.

Secondly, many private and company pension schemes have made a similar mistake. They haven't put aside enough money to pay future pensioners as much as they have been promised.

Thirdly, people in the UK are having fewer children and are living longer. More old people means the state will have to find more cash to pay them a pension. Less young people means less tax will be collected to help pick up the pensions bill.

You can see why it is called the pensions crisis!

Save yourself!

The pensions crisis, like the damage we are doing to the environment, or terrorism, is going to be something you hear a lot about as you grow older.

The only way to be certain you don't get caught up in it is to make sure that by the time you come to retire you are rich enough not to have to worry.

Free money

Happily, it isn't all bad news when it comes to pensions. In order to encourage you to save for your retirement, the state will top up any money you put into a pension plan. They do this through the tax system. In practical terms, it means that if you pay income tax at, say, 22%, every £1 you put into your pension plan will only cost you 78p. If you pay income tax at 40%, every £1 you put into your pension plan will only cost you 60p. This tax break is, basically, free money.

What's the difference between a pension plan and a savings plan?

A pension or retirement plan is a way of saving money specifically for your retirement. What makes it different from an ordinary savings plan is that you will receive help from the taxman (see above). In exchange, however, access to your savings will be restricted. How restricted? Well, it will vary, but typically you won't be able to touch any of the money you have saved until you reach a minimum age (usually 55) – and even then you won't be able to get your hands on all of it as a tax-free lump sum. For this reason you shouldn't put all your savings into your retirement plan when you are young.

Developing a pension plan

You may be wondering exactly how you should set about the business of saving for your retirement. The answer is you need to develop a plan. A good plan might be to:

→ build up an emergency fund of cash
→ save enough money to use as a deposit to buy a home
→ (once you have savings and you've started to buy your home) start a pension plan
→ aim to have your home loan paid off as soon as possible – well before you plan to retire.

Choosing a pension plan

Choosing a pension plan is a complicated business. It will depend on a huge number of issues, including:

→ whether you work for yourself or someone else

→ whether your employer is going to arrange a pension for you
→ the value of your employer's pension
→ what you are entitled to from the state
→ how well off you are
→ when you want to retire
→ how much money you will need when you retire.

When the time comes, you should definitely take professional advice.

Although a pension plan has a lot of extra rules because of the tax savings it offers, in most other ways it is like any sort of investment. The money you put into your pension plan will be invested in anything from stocks and shares to property.

Don't be an ostrich

If you want to build up enough wealth to make sure you can give up work at a reasonable age and never have to worry about money, then don't forget about pension planning. And, in particular, don't act like an ostrich when it comes to the pensions crisis. To guarantee yourself a comfortable retirement you need to start planning early.

HOW TO RETIRE EARLY AND RICH

1	With a little thought – and planning – you could easily be rich enough to stop working while you are still young.
2	The sooner you start planning for your retirement, the cheaper, faster and easier it will be.

18 Money help and where to find it

There are lots of people you can turn to if you want help with your money.

In fact, if you announce you are looking for financial advice, you will quickly find yourself knee-deep in experts offering you assistance.

Finding someone both knowledgeable and trustworthy to advise you, however, is not easy.

There are various reasons for this, but it boils down to the fact that almost every expert is also a salesperson.

Just because someone is interested in selling you something doesn't mean he or she won't be of use to you. Money experts have to make a living, after all, like anyone else.

But it will pay you to be cautious.

What help do you actually need?

Before looking for help, you should decide what your problem actually is.

Some problems are very specific, such as:

→ finding the money to go to university
→ wanting the cheapest loan to buy a car
→ needing a safe home for your savings.

Other problems are more complicated and might involve:

→ getting out of debt
→ investing a lump sum for the best growth
→ choosing the right insurance protection.

You may also want more general advice, such as how to plan all your finances to best advantage.

Do your homework

Once you have worked out what sort of money help you are looking for, you should do a bit of homework.

Let's look at a couple of examples.

Ellen is looking for a loan to buy a car, so she:

→ visits several high-street banks and building societies and picks up leaflets for car loans and checks what rates they are offering
→ looks on the Internet to see what direct deals are available
→ checks the 'best buy' columns of the newspaper (or online) to see what the cheapest deals in the market are.

Before she speaks to anyone about her needs she has a broad idea about the sort of products available.

Harry has got himself into debt and is having trouble making his monthly repayments, so he:

→ visits his local library to see what books they have on the subject
→ looks on the Internet for tips
→ requests information from various charities offering help to people in debt.

Before he looks for advice he has a broad idea about the different options open to him.

Don't be a (knee) jerk

Most people will spend a lot of time shopping for something they want to buy – whether it is a CD, clothes, a computer or a car – but no time at all shopping for financial products such as loans or insurance. What's more, they make one-off financial decisions. 'Oh, I am buying a home: I'd better get a mortgage.' This knee-jerk approach to money is very expensive. If you want the right product for your needs, and if you don't want to waste your cash, then plan ahead.

Money experts come in all shapes and sizes

Money experts come in all shapes and sizes. Here is a quick guide to who they are and what they do.

Who: People working behind the counter in banks, building societies and other financial institutions.
What: They will have limited knowledge – mostly about the products and services their employer offers, which they will try and sell to you.

Who: The more senior managers and salespeople employed by banks, building societies and other financial institutions.
What: They should be quite knowledgeable. Naturally, however, they will try and steer you to a product or service offered by their employer.

Who: Telesales staff who arrange insurance and other quotes by telephone.
What: They will probably have very limited knowledge. All they want is to sell you their employer's product.

Who: Salespeople who work for one particular financial institution – such as an insurance company – or for a handful of such institutions.
What: Whatever knowledge they have is likely to be useless to you because they are out to sell you products supplied by their employer.

Who: Independent Financial Advisers (IFAs) trained to advise you about all aspects of your finances.
What: They should be knowledgeable and are obliged, by law, to give you the 'best' advice.

Who: Chartered Accountants trained to advise you about all aspects of your tax and finances.
What: They should be very knowledgeable and are professionally qualified.

Who: Experts working for charities and non-profit-making organisations whose only interest is in helping you.

What: They are a very useful source of advice and there is no chance of them trying to sell you anything.

Get the right person for the job

Here are some tips to make sure you get the right person for the job:

If you know exactly what you need ...
If you know exactly what you need – such as a bank account or car insurance – then just search out the best deal and buy direct.

If you have a problem ...
If you have a problem – such as too much debt – then you should talk to one of the charities or non-profit-making organisations listed at the end of this chapter.

If you want reliable advice ...
If you want reliable, expert advice and money planning, then your best option is to talk to an Independent Financial Adviser. You'll find some tips in the special section below.

Three things to look out for

Here are three things you want in an adviser.

1. You want them to be really knowledgeable. He or she

MONEY HELP AND WHERE TO FIND IT

> should have proper qualifications. He or she should
> also have experience.
> **2.** You want them to be independent. He or she
> shouldn't work for just one financial institution or
> even just a few financial institutions. He or she should
> be free to give you the best advice.
> **3.** You want them to be trustworthy. He or she should be
> officially recognised (the term is 'authorised') by law
> to advise you. This means they must be 'regulated' (in
> other words, closely watched) by the Financial Services
> Authority (FSA).

How to make sure you get the 'best' advice

The only place to go for impartial money advice is an Independent Financial Adviser (IFA) authorised by (in plain English, supervised by) the Financial Services Authority (FSA). An IFA has to pass a lot of exams to prove he or she understands every aspect of personal finance. He or she must have a really detailed knowledge of insurance, loans, mortgages, investments and banking. What's more, by law, he or she must give you something called 'best advice'. This means that he or she must guide you to the best solution for your needs.

IFAs usually don't charge for their services but get paid for introducing your business to a financial institution. For instance, if an IFA arranges some insurance for you, the insurance company will pay him or her commission (basically an amount of money linked to how much you have to spend on the insurance). However, some IFAs will agree to give you back this commission in exchange for an hourly fee.

You should never, ever take advice from someone who isn't authorised by the FSA.

Free advice!

There is plenty of free advice available:

→ charitable and not-for-profit organisations like Citizens Advice
→ magazines and books available from any library
→ articles in newspapers
→ on the Internet
→ from the government and also from the Financial Services Authority.

Some useful sources of information and help

Citizens Advice will provide you with free legal and financial help. Their website (www.adviceguide.org.uk) is packed with useful information, or look in the telephone book for your nearest branch.

Which? is a registered charity that helps consumers. It publishes a range of magazines and books – often available in public libraries – and there is also lots of information on their website (www.which.co.uk).

The government has created a special website (www.direct.gov.uk) to help you find information about your rights (as well as the law) quickly and easily.

The Financial Services Authority is in charge of policing the financial services industry and also provides lots of useful information on their website (www.fsa.gov.uk).

Moneyfacts (www.moneyfacts.co.uk) is one of several websites that will guide you to the best bank account, best loan or other financial product.

Ask Self (www.AskSelf.co.uk) is my own website. It includes lots of extra articles – including one on starting your own business – together with a competition and study notes.

1	Do your homework before you buy any financial product – it will save you a great deal of money.
2	If you have any money problems or questions, make the local Citizens Advice Bureau your first port of call. The service is excellent and free.

Index

Picture Acknowledgements

The publishers would like to thank Corbis for permission
to reproduce the photographs in this book.